ENDORSEMENTS

Ellen Rogin, CPA, CFP®

New York Times bestselling author of *Picture Your Prosperity*

> "Joyce Marter has created a powerful and practical guide for anyone ready to expand their prosperity from the inside out. *The Financial Mindset Fix Workbook* beautifully bridges emotional well-being and financial growth, offering thoughtful exercises that invite deep self-reflection and real transformation. Joyce's compassionate and insightful approach helps readers understand how mindset and money are inseparable, and how healing one helps the other flourish. This is a must-have companion for anyone ready to create a healthier, more abundant relationship with money and life."

Kathleen Burns Kingsbury, MA, CPCC

Founder, KBK Wealth Connection; Author of *Breaking Money Silence®*

> "*The Financial Mindset Fix* is a comprehensive guide to living an abundant life, drawing on the author's clinical expertise and personal experiences. The companion workbook is a valuable addition, as it helps readers take action and change their relationship with money. That is really what mindset work is all about!"

Bill Cates, CSP, CPAE

Coauthor of *The Hidden Heist – Stop Robbing Yourself of Lasting Wealth*

> "*The Financial Mindset Fix* by Joyce Marter jump started my journey toward a healthier relationship with money. The companion workbook is a brilliant addition to this important work, because rather than just thinking about 'the work' I'm taking action."

Bill Laipple, CFP®

Managing Partner, Stonebridge Wealth Management

> "This workbook is a natural extension of *The Financial Mindset Fix*, turning powerful ideas into practical results. Through clear prompts and step-by-step exercises, it helps readers uncover their deepest values, set authentic goals, and take confident action. It's an accessible, repeatable system for building not just wealth, but genuine peace of mind."

Colleen Bowler, CFP®

C&J Innovations, LLC

> "In my years as a top-tier financial advisor, I learned that no financial plan sticks without the right mindset. That's why Joyce Marter's *Financial Mindset Fix Workbook* is so powerful. She offers simple, repeatable practices—like identifying limiting money beliefs, setting healthy boundaries, and turning goals into habits—that help clients follow through and build lasting change. This workbook is a practical, inspiring companion to any financial strategy and partnership."

Tim Kenny, CPA, CMA, CVA & Certified Profit First Professional

President, Kenny & Kenny

> "I've had the privilege of working with Joyce Marter as her CPA for more than a decade; and I've witnessed firsthand the wisdom, perseverance, and authenticity which lead to her much deserving success as a business owner and mother. *The Financial Mindset Fix* has been an incredible resource for many of our clients, helping them connect their financial habits to their overall well-being. This companion workbook is one of the best tools I've seen for cultivating holistic success—integrating mental wellness, purpose, connection, and financial prosperity."

Susan Frew, CSP

"America's AI for Business Expert"

> "This workbook is a roadmap to genuine financial wellness. Believe me, I know this personally. It's a truth acknowledged by top economic experts, clinical psychologists, and success strategists alike: your financial health is inseparable from your mental and emotional health. For years, people have focused on the external tools of budgeting, saving, and investing, only to find that no financial plan truly 'sticks' without the right internal foundation—the right mindset. Joyce Marter has created this powerful and practical guide for anyone ready to expand their prosperity from the inside out."

Adam L. Saenz, Ph.D., A.B.P.P., D.Min

CEO, Oakwood Counseling

> "Many thanks to Joyce Marter for creating a financial resource that is both clinically sound and readily applicable. This work dives effectively into the underlying psychology of one of the most important relationships in our life: our relationship with money."

Jaclyn Bradley, MSOD

Advisor Transformation Coach, Mindshift Financial Coaching

> "I've spent my career helping financial advisors address the human side of money because I understand this truth: your financial health is inseparable from your mental and emotional health. Joyce Marter's *Financial Mindset Fix Workbook* is the resource I wish everyone had — practical exercises rooted in psychology that help you understand and transform your deepest money beliefs. This isn't just another budgeting guide; it's a roadmap to genuine financial wellness."

Jennifer Froemel, LCPC, CIMHP

Owner, Innovative Counseling Partners, PLLC

"As a trauma-informed group practice owner, I was concerned about how often our clinicians and clients struggled to engage in meaningful discussions around finances. I asked Joyce to provide a full-day training on how the exercises in *The Financial Mindset Fix Workbook* can help both clinicians and clients move beyond financial trauma—and the results have been remarkable. I've witnessed firsthand the transformation these exercises create. Since that training, we now assess for financial trauma as part of our client intake process. These tools are truly transformative!"

AmondaRose Igoe

Speaking Success Strategist and Creator of ShePowered® Speaking

"I absolutely loved *The Financial Mindset Fix Workbook!* It's clear, encouraging, and full of practical insights that really make you think differently about money. The exercises are simple yet powerful, and you can feel the heart and wisdom behind every page. It's like having a mindset coach cheering you on with every step."

THE FINANCIAL MINDSET FIX WORKBOOK:
A Mental Fitness Program for an Abundant Life

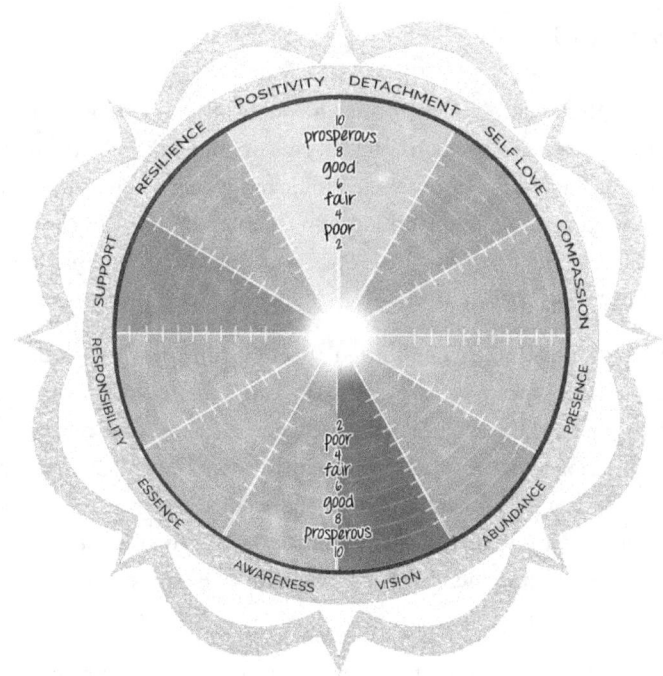

By

JOYCE MARTER, LCPC, CSP®

LEADERSHIP
Thoughtful. Relevant Leaders From Around The World
BOOKS

THE FINANCIAL MINDSET FIX WORKBOOK:

A Mental Fitness Program for an Abundant Life

JOYCE MARTER, LCPC, CSP®

TABLE OF CONTENTS

INTRODUCTION

The Wheel Exercise Tutorial

The wheel exercises are self-evaluation tools that help you realize where your strengths and weaknesses lie in a given area. Don't worry about your scores—we are all works in progress. Since you'll be doing the wheel exercises throughout this program, you can turn to this tutorial for a refresher. Completing the wheel exercise is easy. After you go through it once, you'll be a pro. And if you become discouraged because there is still progress to be made, always remember we are looking for progress, not perfection.

Each wheel exercise begins with a set of questions. After you read a question, simply rate yourself on the following scale: Poor (1-3), Fair (4-5), Good (6-7), Prosperous (8-10).

Each wheel diagram contains a set of spokes, similar to the spokes on a bicycle wheel. After you answer each wheel exercise question, chart your answer on the wheel. Find the spoke that matches the label of the question. Then, simply place a dot on the spoke next to the number that corresponds with your answer. For example, if you rated yourself a 3, put a dot at the 3 mark on the spoke.

After scoring yourself on every spoke, connect the dots to create a circle. Note that the higher a number is, the closer it is to the outer section of the wheel, while lower scores are more toward the middle. To get an idea of how it looks, see the Financial Health Wheel Example below.

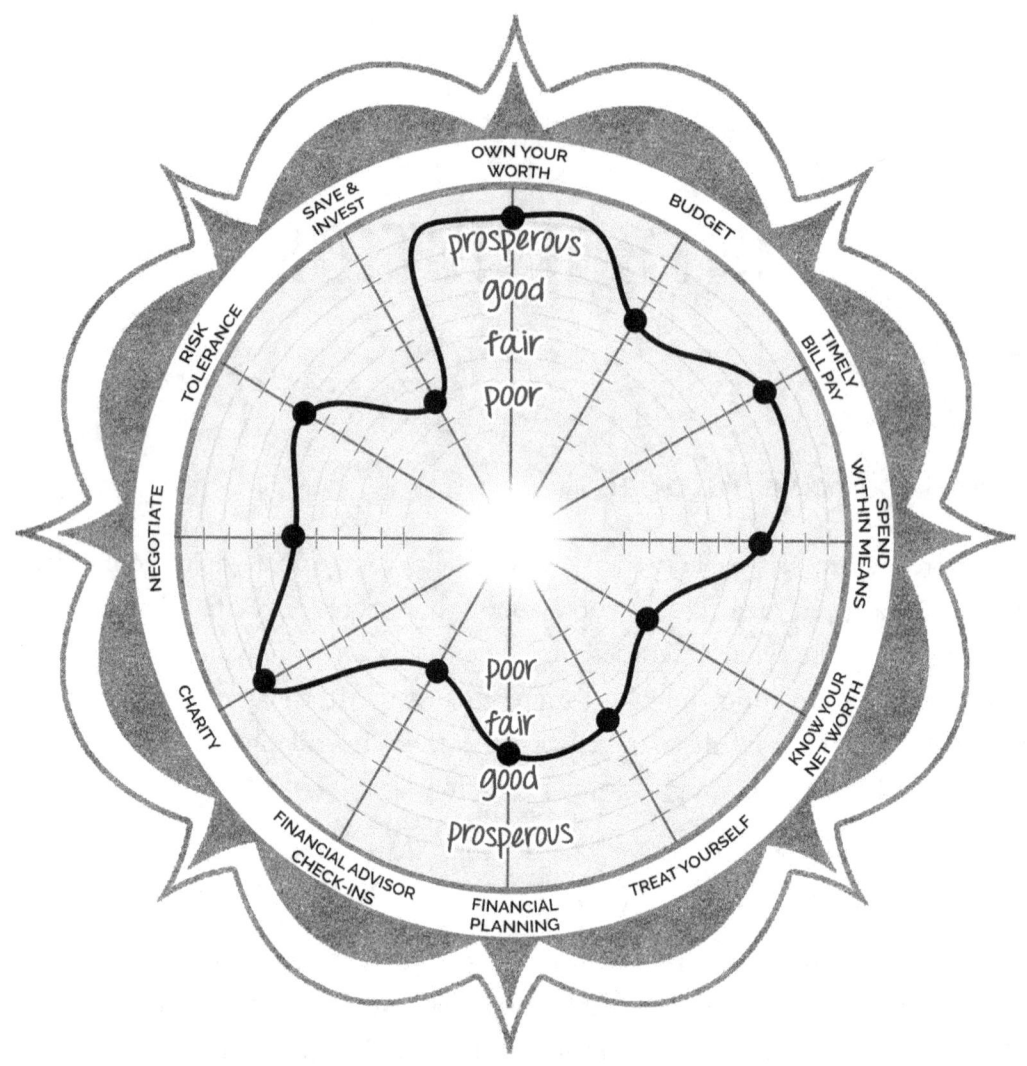

The Financial Wheel Example

The "dents" on the wheel represent areas where this person scored lower. This wheel was filled out by someone who doesn't have much when it comes to Save & Invest, so she scored low in that area, but she scored high when it came to Charity. This program provides the opportunity to begin working on these dents, or areas of deficit, today.

To get a base reading on how you currently handle finances, you're going to start by completing The Financial Health Wheel. Throughout this program, you'll dive into different aspects of your financial health, then revisit this same exercise at the end of the book to see all the progress you've made!

EXERCISE #1: THE FINANCIAL HEALTH WHEEL

(Time to complete: 20 minutes)

Date: _____

Rate your response after each question using a number from the following scale:

Poor (1-3), Fair (4-5), Good (6-7), Prosperous (8-10)									
Poor			**Fair**			**Good**		**Prosperous**	
1	2	3	4	5	6	7	8	9	10

Own Your Worth: How deserving of greater financial prosperity do you feel?

(Abundance) _____

Budget: How aware are you of your earnings and spending? Do you check your budget and cash flow at least once a month, live within your budget, and avoid slipping into financial denial?

(Awareness) _____

Timely Bill Pay: Not paying bills on time can mean late fees and dings to your credit. How do you rate yourself on organizing and paying bills on time? (Responsibility) _____

Spend Within Means: Do you practice mindful spending? How well do you spend within your limits so you do not accrue debt? (Presence) _____

Know Your Net Worth: Net worth is the calculation of all assets (balances of all your bank accounts, value investments, and property) minus your liabilities (balances on credit cards, loans, and mortgages). How do you rate yourself at knowing your approximate net worth at any given time? (Essence) _____

Treat Yourself Within Means: How good are you at treating yourself within means when you feel you deserve it? (Self-Love) _____

Financial Planning: When it comes to your financial health, including paying off student loans or credit card debt and saving to buy a home, your kids' college, or your retirement, how would you rate yourself? (Vision) _____

Financial Advisor Check-Ins: How good are you about meeting with a financial advisor once or twice a year to keep on track? (Support) _____

Joyce Marter, LCPC, CSP®

Charity: How good are you at supporting causes that are meaningful to you in a doable way? (Compassion) _____

Negotiate: Negotiating includes asking for better pay or benefits, discussing the price of major purchases or contracts, and bartering services when possible in order to get a deal. How good are you when it comes to negotiating? (Positivity) _____

Risk Tolerance: When you have adequate insurance in place, it becomes easier to detach from the outcome. How would you rate yourself when it comes to having the proper amount of insurance for your health, car, house/apartment, business, and even life? (Detachment) _____

Save & Invest: Having at least three to six months of expenses in your savings and investments such as an IRA for your future, is a good rule of thumb. How would you rate yourself when it comes to saving and investing for a rainy day? (Resilience) _____

Chart your responses on The Financial Health Wheel. Start at the top of the wheel. For each spoke, ask yourself if you're Poor, Prosperous, or somewhere in between. Put a dot on the spoke next to the number that corresponds with your answer. Now, continue going around the wheel and after scoring yourself on every spoke, connect the dots to create a circle. Remember, just be honest with your responses.

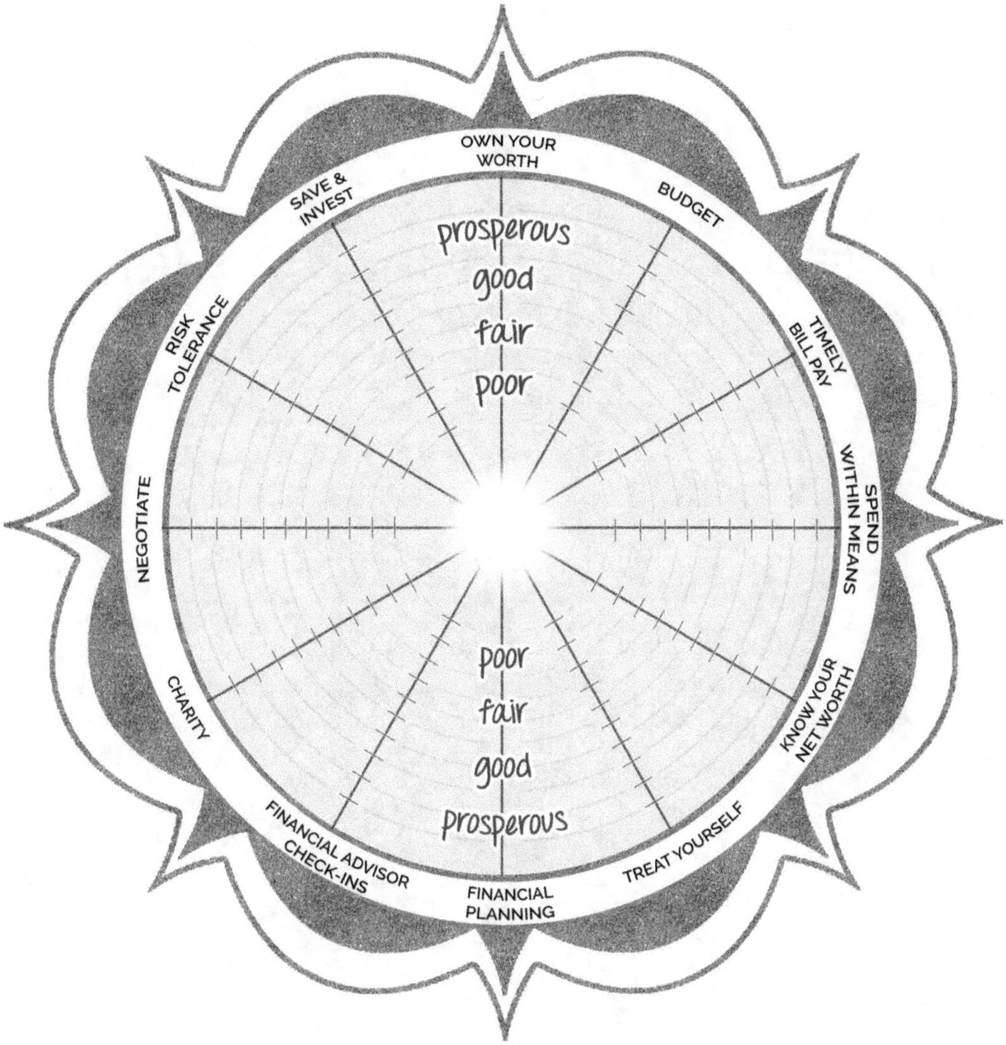

OWN YOUR WORTH
BUDGET
TIMELY BILL PAY
SPEND WITHIN MEANS
KNOW YOUR NET WORTH
TREAT YOURSELF
FINANCIAL PLANNING
FINANCIAL ADVISOR CHECK-INS
CHARITY
NEGOTIATE
RISK TOLERANCE
SAVE & INVEST
prosperous
good
fair
poor
poor
fair
good
prosperous

The Financial Health Wheel

Date your wheel so you can reference it when you reassess your financial health at the conclusion of the program. Congratulations! You have now completed your first exercise in this program. It gives you a good reading of your financial health now, before starting the program. Even if you rate yourself pretty well when it comes to your finances, you will learn how to continue to expand and improve your well-being and financial health.

CHAPTER -

Abundance

EXERCISE #1: THERAPY SESSION NUMBER 1

(Time to complete: 20 minutes)

Imagine you are in my office for your first therapy session. We'll explore how your life experiences with money may have shaped and molded your relationship with money today. Write your responses to the following questions below:

➤ What cultural, religious, and family belief systems about money were you taught?

_____

_____

_____

_____

➤ What are your attitudes and beliefs about people with a lot of money? With very little money?

_____

_____

_____

_____

➢ Growing up, did you notice expectations surrounding money were different for males than females, for the young versus the old, for different types of professions, or differing expectations resulting from ethnic or racial discrimination?

_____

_____

_____

_____

➢ How has this impacted your financial life today?

_____

_____

_____

_____

➢ What do you think of when you hear the word *money*? For me, it was stress, which is negative. Are your thoughts positive or negative when you hear the word *money?*

_____

_____

_____

_____

➢ Do you set income ceilings for yourself? If so, what have they been, and what is holding you back from breaking through those ceilings?

_____

_____

_____

_____

➤ Do you feel truly capable and deserving of having an abundance of money and other resources? If not, why?

_____

_____

_____

_____

Now, pretend you are reviewing your responses with me. Highlight the top three ways of thinking that might be preventing you from living an abundant life. For example, if you were taught that rich people are bad or men should earn more money than women, ask yourself how might you reframe those beliefs to receive abundance and take better care of yourself, your loved ones, and the world around you? Write this out. This is the type of work you need to do to start embracing The Financial Mindset Fix.

EXERCISE #2: LOOK AT YOUR FINANCIAL SELF IN THE MIRROR

(Time to complete: 20 minutes)

Answer the following questions:

➤ If your finances were a person, what would you name them?

_____

_____

_____

_____

➤ How would they look and feel?

_____

_____

_____

_____

➤ What is the nature of your relationship?

_____

_____

_____

_____

➤ What's the connection between who you see in the mirror and your financial self-worth?

_____

_____

_____

_____

EXERCISE #3: EXAMINE YOUR SELF-WORTH

(Time to complete: 10 minutes; lifetime practice)

Answer the following questions:

➤ Imagine somebody who believes in you (like your best friend, colleague, or mother) is asked to describe your unique gifts and strengths. What would they say?

_____

_____

_____

_____

➤ Describe a time when you pleasantly surprised yourself on what you were able to accomplish. How did that feel? What did you learn from that experience that could translate to other aspects of your life?

_____

_____

_____

_____

➤ When do you feel the most valuable? In which relationships? Why?

_____

_____

_____

_____

➤ Write about a time when you felt you were compensated appropriately for a job well done. How did that come to be? Did that opportunity fall in your lap, or did you welcome it somehow? What can you learn from this experience?

_____

Joyce Marter, LCPC, CSP®

_____

_____

_____

_____

Your self-worth reflects how much abundance you are willing to let into your life.

EXERCISE #4: SYNERGIZE FOR SUCCESS

(Time to complete: 10 minutes; lifetime practice)

Answer the following questions:

➢ With whom do you feel competitive? How might feeling competitive be hurting you?

_____

_____

_____

_____

➢ How do your competitors inspire you? What can you learn from them? Identify the blessings.

_____

_____

_____

_____

➢ How can you invite more collaboration into your life?

_____

_____

_____

_____

➢ How will shifting from competition to collaboration help you welcome greater abundance?

_____

_____

_____

_____

Joyce Marter, LCPC, CSP®

EXERCISE #5: RECORD AND REWIRE YOUR THINKING

(Time to complete: 15 minutes; lifetime practice)

Cognitive behavioral therapy (CBT) helps people become aware of and change their negative thought patterns—or in simpler terms, to stop their stinkin' thinkin'. CBT uses thought records or thought dairies as tools to identify and change negative thinking patterns to make thoughts more neutral or positive.

You will be using the following thought record chart. Think back to the last couple of weeks when you were emotionally distressed about something, especially your financial life, and write it down in your chart. I've included some example responses to get you started.

Situation	Thought	Emotion	Behavior	Alternate Thought
Your coworker received the promotion instead of you.	"I suck."	Anger, sadness, shame	Sulky and passive-aggressive	"There will be a better opportunity for me in the future."

By changing the thought from negative to positive, the emotions you feel may be empowerment, peace, trust, or hope. These emotions lead to behaviors that are more celebratory of others' successes. Thought records are a lifelong tool that can change your thinking from negative to positive.

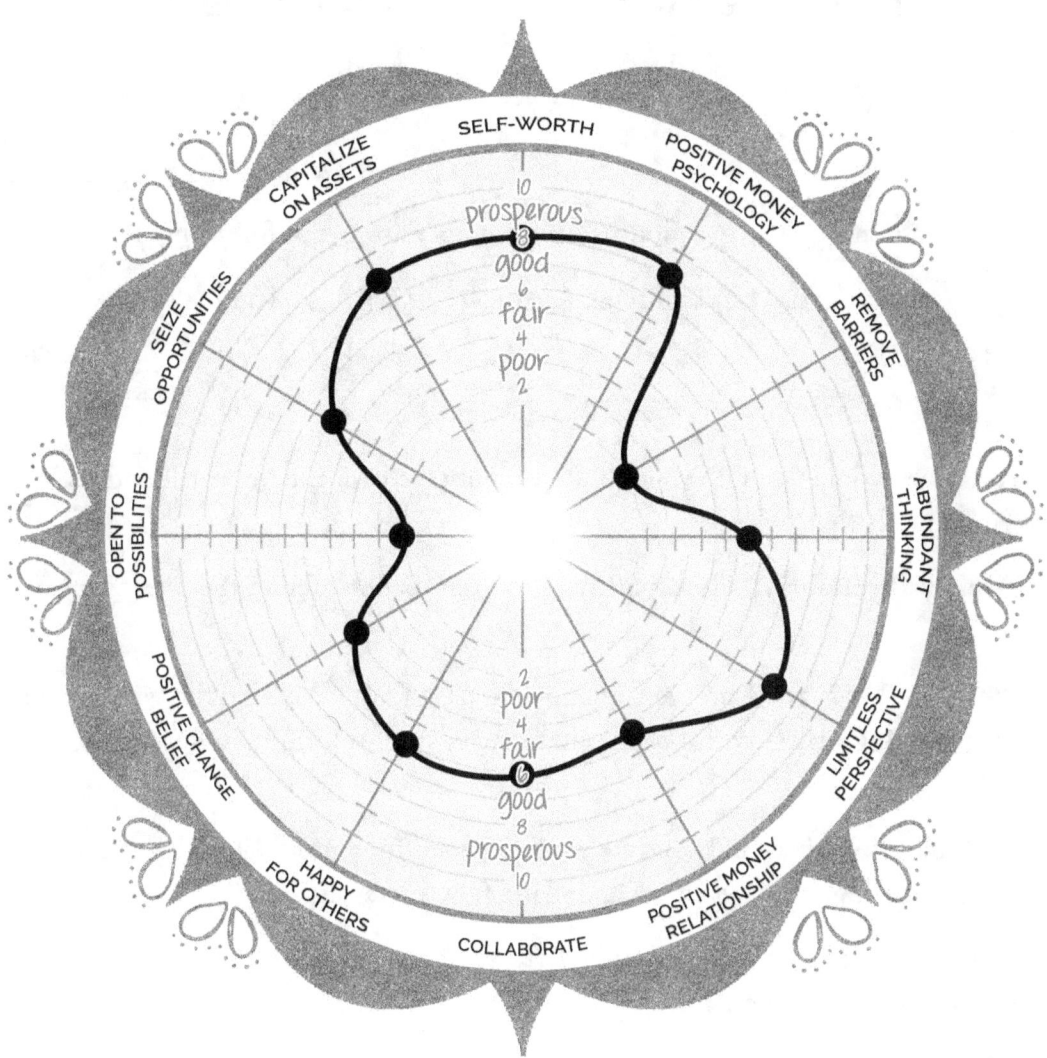

The Abundance Wheel Example

This wheel was filled out by someone who wasn't very Open to Possibilities for herself, so she scored low in that area; but she scored high when it came to Happiness for Others. The "dents" on the wheel represent areas where she scored lower. This program provides the opportunity to begin working these dents, or areas of deficit, today. With significant areas of deficiency, your wheel may look more like a "constellation" than a circle, and that's okay! Revisit this exercise as you work through The Financial Mindset Fix program. To get a base reading on where abundance shows up in your life currently, complete the Abundance Wheel.

Joyce Marter, LCPC, CSP®

EXERCISE #6: THE ABUNDANCE WHEEL

(Time to complete: 20 minutes)

Date: _____

Rate your response after each question using a number from the following scale:

Poor (1-3), Fair (4-5), Good (6-7), Prosperous (8-10)			
Poor	**Fair**	**Good**	**Prosperous**
1 2 3	4 5	6 7	8 9 10

Self-Worth: How would you rate your ability to embrace your innate worth and feel deserving of prosperity and all that is good? _____

Positive Money Psychology: How positive are your beliefs about the meaning of money? _____

Remove Barriers: How good are you at moving past guilty feelings for wanting more and replacing self-limiting beliefs with positive statements that welcome the flow of money to you? _____

Abundant Thinking: How would you rate yourself when it comes to abundant thinking instead of scarcity thinking and trusting in an abundant flow of resources? _____

Limitless Perspective: How well are you able to see past limits (other than ethical) and think big about your life and financial future? _____

Positive Money Relationship: How would you rate yourself at having an attentive and nurturing relationship with money? _____

Collaborate: When it comes to working together rather than working in competition, how would you rate yourself? _____

Happy for Others: While celebrating the joys and successes of others, how convinced are you that this does not mean there is less for you? _____

Positive Change Belief: Do you believe that even if life is difficult now or your finances are in bad shape, things can improve? _____

Open to Possibilities: Instead of seeing roadblocks, how willing are you to look at new ways of doing things so your work, finances, and life can grow and flourish? _____

Seize Opportunities: How good are you at accepting invitations, attending events, classes, online seminars, e-courses, and other opportunities extended to you? _____

Capitalize on Assets: How would you rate yourself at utilizing the gifts, talents, and resources that are available to you? _____

Chart your responses on The Abundance Wheel. Let's start at the top: are you Poor, Prosperous, or somewhere in between when it comes to Self-Worth? Put a dot on the spoke next to the number that corresponds with your answer. Now, continue going around the wheel and after scoring yourself on every spoke, connect the dots to create a circle. Don't worry about your scores. Just be honest.

The Abundance Wheel

To see where you are at when it comes to abundance, answer the following questions:

➤ Where are the three biggest "dents" in your wheel?

_____

_____

_____

_____

➤ What do you see as the biggest obstacles to achieving a Prosperous rating in these three areas?

_____

_____

_____

_____

➤ Any ideas on how you can transcend those limitations?

_____

_____

_____

_____

CHAPTER -

Awareness

EXERCISE #1: THERAPY SESSION NUMBER 2

(Time to complete: 20 minutes)

Imagine you are back in my office for a second session, where we are working on promoting your awareness. As I ask you the following questions, write your responses below..

➢ What did my story bring up for you?

_____

_____

_____

_____

➢ How did your family impact your mental health? Your financial health?

_____

_____

_____

➤ Can you think about a time in your life when self-awareness helped improve both your well-being and your finances?

_____

_____

_____

_____

The following are some examples of common roles in families, as well as how they end up impacting one's career and financial life:

Hero or Golden Child: is a high achiever person and the pride of the family. They are often good leaders who are goal oriented and self- disciplined but may lack the ability to relax or allow others to be right or in charge. Heroes tend to become business owners and business leaders but may struggle in some of their personal relationships because of their tendency to be bossy or domineering.

Scapegoat or Black Sheep: Family members may feel this person has problems—including mental health, addiction, social or financial issues. The scapegoat may show the signs and symptoms of underlying family problems. Their strengths may include a sense of humor, vulnerability, and authenticity. They tend to struggle to transition into adulthood and achieve less success in their career and finances.

Good Child: is the passive, subservient child who avoids being a problem. They tend to be flexible and easygoing, but lack direction, are fearful of making decisions, and follow others without questioning. They may end up being taken for granted in relationships or working in support roles which tend to be lower paying.

Mascot or Clown: These people use humor to diffuse conflict and may not feel free to express their true selves. They tend to have emotionally immature relationships that lack a deeper intimacy, and may end up working in sales or entertainment, which can be lucrative for some, but challenging for many.

Mediator: Mediators work to keep peace in the family system and may also be a rescuer. They act as a communicator or buffer, which may or may not be healthy for them depending on how well received or effective their efforts are. Mediators may work as attorneys, real estate brokers, or middle managers.

Nurturer: These people provide emotional support and stability in a balanced and healthy way. They can also be a mediator and may work with children or in education.

Rescuer: This person takes care of other family member's problems, often to relieve their own anxiety. They tend to experience guilt and are prone to codependency and detrimental caretaking at their own expense. They may work in helping professions as a therapist, nurse, or paramedic. Overall, helping professionals do not realize their true earning potential as they tend to view their finances as being outside of their control and accept the notion that they will not make much money.

Cheerleader: These people provide encouragement and support to others while taking care of their own needs and having a positive influence on others. They may work in marketing or leadership roles to motivate customers or staff.

Thinker: These people are objective, logical, and rational, but may find it difficult to emotionally connect with others. They may be drawn to science, medicine, mathematics, and have difficulty with the people skills needed for networking and business development.

Truth Teller: This person says it like it is. They communicate the information that is needed, but others may not appreciate their advice. This role can be a real strength when coupled with the qualities of a nurturer or cheerleader. Journalism or law are natural career choices for these people.

You may have played more than one of these roles in your family of origin. Hang onto the good parts of your roles, but shift whatever is no longer serving you.

EXERCISE #2: IDENTIFY YOUR DEFAULT ROLE

(Time to complete: 20 minutes)

➤ Reflect on your role in your family of origin. Write down two to three roles from the family systems theory that you most identify with and explain why.

_____

_____

_____

_____

➤ How might each of these roles be affecting your personal relationships or work life?

_____

_____

_____

_____

➤ How might each of these roles be affecting your finances?

_____

_____

_____

_____

➤ Identify two strengths and two challenges of each role.

_____

_____

_____

_____

➤ For each role, describe one change you would like to make to enhance your relationships and one change you would like to make to enhance your professional life or finances.

_____

_____

_____

_____

EXERCISE #3: DROP YOUR DEFENSES

(Time to complete: 20 minutes; lifetime practice)

Write about a time you used some of the following defenses.

- Denial

- Displacement

- Sublimation

- Projection

- Intellectualization

- Rationalization

- Regression

- Reaction Formation

If you are having a hard time coming up with an example, ask a trusted confidant like a close friend or family member, your partner, or therapist for help. Then, answer the following questions:

➤ How did you use those defenses to justify your behaviors or decisions?

_____

_____

_____

_____

➤ How were those behaviors or decisions harmful to your mental health or relationships?

_____

_____

_____

_____

➢ Do you think it's possible that defense mechanisms like denial may have played a role in your financial issues?

_____

_____

_____

_____

➢ How might things have turned out differently if you dropped the defenses?

_____

_____

_____

_____

EXERCISE #4: CHECK UP ON YOUR MENTAL HEALTH

(Time to complete: 20 minutes; lifetime practice)

Answer the following questions:

➢ What is your family's history of mental health problems, substance abuse, or addiction? Do you have a genetic predisposition to any of these issues?

_____

_____

_____

_____

➢ What mental health warning signs do you recognize in yourself? Has anybody ever expressed concern to you about this?

_____

_____

_____

_____

➢ Have you or anybody else been concerned about your substance use or addictive behaviors?

_____

_____

_____

_____

➢ Have your work or finances been negatively impacted by your mental health, substance use, or addiction issues? If so, how?

_____

_____

_____

EXERCISE #5: CHECK YOUR REALITY BY BUDGETING

(Time to complete: Times vary depending on how organized your finances are; this is a lifetime practice)

The following checklist includes the six steps you need to follow to create a simple budget. Tackle the steps one at a time and check the boxes once you've completed the task. I suggest creating a spreadsheet on your computer so you can easily track and make adjustments as needed.

Note that some of the boxes under each step might not apply to you. For example, you may not have a student loan balance, so just leave that box blank under Step One.

Step One: Gather your financial statements. This will be helpful as you calculate your monthly expenses in Step Three.

- Bank statements
- Credit card statements
- Student loan balances
- Other loans
- Investment accounts
- Utility bills
- Cell phone statements
- Any other information that identifies monthly averages of income and expenses

Step Two: Tally your sources of monthly income.

- Paycheck—If taxes are automatically deducted, use the take-home amount. If you're self-employed, deduct about 20 percent from your take-home pay for taxes.
- Side hustles—Maybe you're an Uber driver, own an Airbnb, or sell health and wellness products on the side.
- Seasonal work
- Bonuses
- Other

Joyce Marter, LCPC, CSP®

Step Three: Create a list of estimated monthly expenses. The financial statements you gathered in Step One will help you calculate this.

- Rent or mortgage
- Car payments
- Groceries
- Auto insurance
- Entertainment
- Gym membership or fitness classes
- Loan payments
- Retirement or college savings
- Professional membership fees (add them up and divide by 12)
- Charitable donations (add them up and divide by 12)
- Vacations, holiday and birthday gifts (add them up and divide by 12)
- Other

Step Four: Break expenses into two categories—fixed and variable.

Fixed expenses are those that are essential and stay relatively the same each month.

- Mortgage or rent
- Car payment
- Cable and/or internet service
- Other

Variable expenses are those that change from month to month

- Groceries
- Dining out
- Credit card payments
- Clothes shopping
- Household shopping
- Other

Total each category in your Excel document.

Step Five: Subtract your total monthly expenses from your total monthly income. If your amount is positive, you are in good shape. This means you can budget to use this excess for paying off your credit cards, student loans, or mortgage, or saving to buy a home or contributing more to your retirement plan. If your amount is negative, it means you need to make some adjustments either by working more, seeking greater compensation, and/or reducing your variable expenses by cutting back on eating out or excessive spending at the salon, spa, or bars!

Step Six: Review your budget weekly or monthly. Review your budget on a regular basis to make sure you're living within your means and staying on track with your financial health. Create a routine, such as every Sunday afternoon, when you (and your partner, if you are in a relationship) compare the budgeted expenses versus what you actually spent. This reveals where you did well and where you need to improve. A good rule of thumb is to spend about 50 percent of your income on fixed expenses, 30 percent on variable expenses, and save at least 20 percent.

By completing this budget checklist, you now have a starting point. Did anything come up that surprised you? Some people feel shame, fear, anxiety, or resistance about creating a budget. Others feel anger or rage because they're making less than they should be because of discrimination based on race, gender, or immigration status. This is normal. I encourage you to honor these understandable feelings, get support from others, and power through. I detest budgeting and it makes me incredibly anxious and fuels shame. Because I care about myself and my financial well-being, I have had to push past this in order to become financially conscious. I encourage you to do the same. Although sticking to a budget is not easy, being aware of what is going on with your finances will empower you to reap financial gain over time.

EXERCISE #6: THE AWARENESS WHEEL

(Time to complete: 20 minutes)

Date: _____

Rate your response after each question using a number from the following scale:

Poor (1-3), Fair (4-5), Good (6-7), Prosperous (8-10)			
Poor	**Fair**	**Good**	**Prosperous**
1 2 3	4 5	6 7	8 9 10

Self-Awareness: How aware are you of your personality characteristics, your strengths and areas of needed growth, and how you impact others? _____

Relational Roles: How aware are you of the roles and patterns you often play in group dynamics—including family and work—and how this impacts your financial success? _____

Unconscious Contracts: How good are you at recognizing possible unspoken agreements? How are they impacting your mental health, work, and finances? _____

Defensive Mechanisms: Are you aware when defenses like denial, rationalization, or projection pop up and impair your well-being and prosperity? _____

Substance Use: How aware are you of your substance use (caffeine, sugar, alcohol, recreational, prescription, and other drug use) and how it impacts your mental, physical, and financial health? (Please note that substance use does not necessarily mean you are a substance abuser or have a substance use disorder, which are disorders that span a wide array of problems arising from substance use.) _____

Addictions: Addiction is the use of substances or engaging in compulsive behaviors that continue despite harmful consequences. Addiction is a treatable, chronic disease that involves interactions between the brain, genetics, the environment, and a person's life experiences.<SS>17</SS> How aware are you of how an addiction to drugs, alcohol, shopping, gaming, or sex has negatively impacted your finances? _____

Traumas: How good are you at recognizing your history of traumas, including financial traumas, and how they might be influencing your mental and financial health? _____

Attachment Style: How aware are you of your attachment style and how it impacts your relationships and your finances? _____

Stressors: Relationship issues, financial challenges, losses, deadlines, projects, and holidays can all increase your stress level and may be negatively impacting your mental health and functioning at work. How would you rate yourself when it comes to figuring out what is stressing you out? _____

Physical Health: How aware are you of your physical health and how that may be impacting other aspects of your life, including mental and financial health? _____

Mental Health: How aware are you of the impact of your stress levels, emotional wellness, and experiences of depression, anxiety, or other mental health issues? _____

Financial Consciousness: When it comes to being aware and understanding your financial reality, how would you rate yourself? Do you combat financial denial by having and living within a budget? _____

Chart your responses on The Awareness Wheel. Let's start at the top: are you Poor, Prosperous, or somewhere in between when it comes to Self-Awareness? Put a dot on the spoke next to the number that corresponds with your answer. Now, continue going around the wheel and after scoring yourself on every spoke, connect the dots to create a circle.

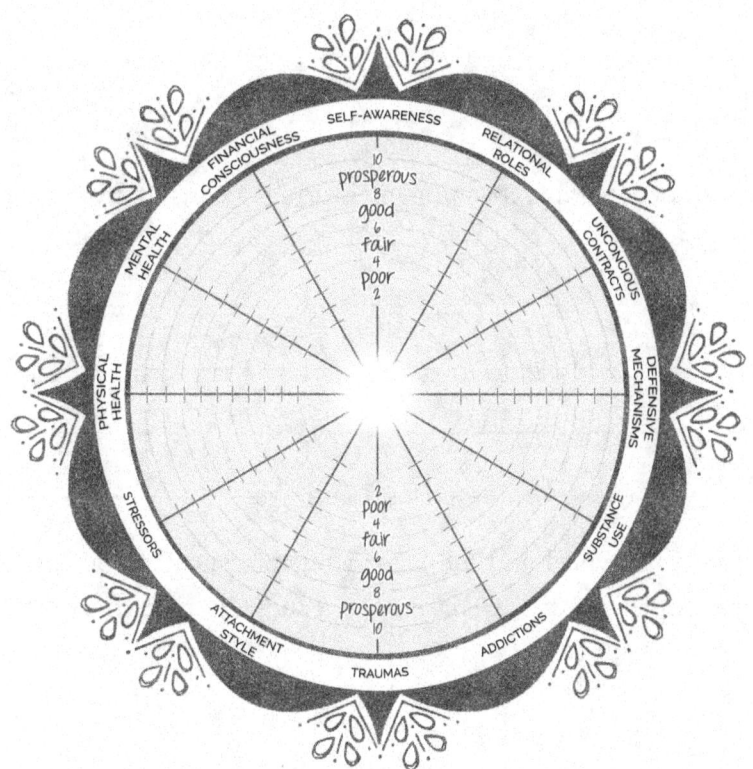

Joyce Marter, LCPC, CSP®

The Awareness Wheel

Don't worry about your scores; just be honest. Continue to practice this mindset just like you would exercise to improve your fitness. Then, answer the following questions:

> ➢ As you look at your completed wheel, where do you see the biggest dents? What are two things you can do better right now in those areas?

_____

_____

_____

_____

> ➢ As you look at the wheel, what three areas of your mental and financial life are you least aware of?

_____

_____

_____

_____

> ➢ Would you consider therapy, coaching, mentoring, a consultation, or training to promote more awareness?

_____

_____

_____

_____

Remember to date your wheel and file it for later reference so you can track your progress over time. Consider completing this exercise once a month or quarterly so you can live more consciously.

CHAPTER - 3

Responsibility

EXERCISE #1: THERAPY SESSION NUMBER 3

(Time to complete: 20 minutes)

Welcome back to my office! This time, we are working on taking responsibility for your life. Write your responses to this session's questions below:

In what ways do you already take responsibility for improving your financial success?

> In what ways do you feel irresponsible when it comes to improving your financial success?

_____

_____

_____

_____

> Do you think you err on the side of shying away from responsibility or taking too much responsibility? What are the effects of these tendencies?

_____

_____

_____

_____

➤ In the past, who have you blamed when you were unhappy, underwent challenges, or experienced setbacks?

_____

_____

_____

_____

➤ How would you feel if you took greater responsibility for yourself, your circumstances, and your finances? What is the hard part about doing that? What are the potential positives?

_____

_____

_____

_____

Review your responses. Instead of taking responsibility for your own life, are you blaming others or making excuses? If so, it's time to call yourself out and take responsibility going forward.

EXERCISE #2: AUTHOR YOUR BEST FUTURE

(Time to complete: 20 minutes)

Answer the following:

➤ Write down the ten primary challenges life has dealt you, including financial challenges.

_____

_____

_____

_____

➤ Write down the ten primary blessings life has provided you, including talents, gifts, support, or resources. Highlight any blessings which may have stemmed from your challenges. For example, you are hardworking because you had to be to survive. How could you utilize your blessings to create a happier and more prosperous life?

_____

_____

_____

_____

➤ Become the author of your future. Write about the next five years and how your life will blossom, personally and financially, by building on all of your blessings and strengths.

_____

_____

_____

_____

➢ How does taking responsibility factor into your successful future?

_____

_____

_____

_____

EXERCISE #3: TAKE AN HONEST LOOK AT YOURSELF

(Time to complete: 10 minutes; lifetime practice)

Answer the following:

> ➤ What do you see as the challenging aspects of your personality? Why? How have they negatively impacted your relationships, career, and/or finances?

_____

_____

_____

_____

> ➤ How do you take ownership of these character traits? How could you do better at managing them?

_____

_____

_____

_____

> ➤ How might speaking in "I-Messages" help your relationships? How are you going to work on this?

_____

_____

_____

_____

EXERCISE #4: TAKE FISCAL RESPONSIBILITY

(Time to complete: 10 minutes; lifetime practice)

Answer the following:

➤ Who or what do you feel is responsible for your current financial situation? How were you impacted?

_____

_____

_____

_____

➤ Now, write about your part in creating your current financial life. Be both honest and gentle with yourself. The goal is for you to take ownership of your role.

_____

_____

_____

_____

➤ You are responsible for your financial life going forward, so it's time to take the reins. How responsible are you in managing your money? Do you have a system and does it work well? Have you incurred any late fees for bill payments within the last twelve months? Write down ways you can increase your financial responsibility—consider software like QuickBooks or free money-management sites like Mint.

_____

_____

_____

_____

EXERCISE #5: THE RESPONSIBILITY WHEEL

(Time to complete: 20 minutes)

Date: _____

Rate your response after each question using a number from the following scale:

Poor (1-3), Fair (4-5), Good (6-7), Prosperous (8-10)									
Poor			**Fair**			**Good**		**Prosperous**	
1	2	3	4	5	6	7	8	9	10

Do Your Part: How willing are you to step up and do the work it takes to succeed in your relationships, work, and finances? _____

Acceptance: How good are you at embracing the hardships you have been dealt, including financial, and not blaming others? _____

Empowerment: How empowered are you to take action to determine your course in life, work, and finances? _____

Own Your Happiness: How good are you at taking responsibility for your attitude and happiness instead of assigning blame to others? _____

Forgive: How good are you at freeing yourself from resentment for any wrongdoings, financial and otherwise? _____

Apologize: When it comes to looking at your mistakes or less than ideal choices, how much responsibility do you take when it comes to the impact on others, work, and your finances?

_____

Integrity: Integrity is being dependable and reliable, following through with commitments, doing what you said you would do, and so forth. How responsible are you when it comes to being honest, ethical, and truthful? _____

Healthy Choices: When it comes to your overall wellness, how good are you at making healthy choices? _____

Manage Money: How responsible are you when it comes to taking ownership of your financial life, paying your debts and bills on time, and taking responsibility for the income you earn and the money you spend? _____

Joyce Marter, LCPC, CSP®

Career Goals: How would you rate yourself when it comes to tending to your professional aspirations? _____

Personal Goals: How would you rate yourself when it comes to tending to your personal aspirations, like health goals, relationship goals, hobbies, and travel? _____

Foster Balance: How would you rate yourself when it comes to balancing your responsibilities to the best of your ability? _____

Chart your responses on The Responsibility Wheel. Start at the top: are you Poor, Prosperous, or somewhere in between when it comes to being able to Do Your Part? Put a dot on the spoke next to the number that corresponds with your answer. Now, continue going around the wheel and after scoring yourself on every spoke, connect the dots to create a circle.

The Responsibility Wheel

Answer the following questions:

> As you look at your completed wheel, where do you see the biggest dents? What do you see as your biggest challenge to improving within these areas?

_____

_____

_____

_____

> How can you address that challenge? Is there anybody who could help you?

_____

_____

_____

_____

> What are three small changes you can make to cultivate more responsibility in both your personal and financial life?

_____

_____

_____

_____

> Consider completing this exercise once a month or quarterly so you can continue to foster responsibility for your success. Remember, aim for progress, not perfection! Date your wheel and file it for later reference so you can track your progress over time.

_____

_____

_____

_____

Presence

EXERCISE #1: THERAPY SESSION NUMBER 4

(Time to complete: 20 minutes)

This session applies mindfulness to your mental and financial health. Write your responses to the following questions:

➤ How has the disease of "being busy" played a role in your life?

_____

_____

_____

_____

➤ What prevents you from being more present?

_____

_____

_____

_____

➤ How might being more present improve your financial wellness?

_____

_____

_____

_____

EXERCISE #2: PUMP THE BREAKS ON BUSYNESS

(Time to complete: 20 minutes; lifetime practice)

Answer the following questions:

➢ Which of the previous suggestions for hopping off the Busy Train do you already do well? How has it helped you be more successful?

_____

_____

_____

_____

➢ On a scale from 1 to 10, how overly busy do you feel? *Totally chill* is a 1 rating while *Totally crazed* is a 10 rating. If you self-scored 3 or less, you are out of danger; 4-6 you are doing well, but there is room for improvement; and 7-10 you are in the *danger zone!*

_____

_____

_____

_____

➢ What three ways do you plan to implement any of the suggestions for hopping off the Busy Train? Tell a friend or colleague and set a time to follow up on your progress next week.

_____

_____

_____

_____

EXERCISE #3: REDIRECT YOUR ATTENTION TO THE HERE AND NOW

(Time to complete: 10 minutes; lifetime practice)

Answer the following:

➢ List three past events or choices that often occupy your mind. Implement being thankful for the lessons learned. For each event, write two valuable lessons you learned. To help you let go, consider forgiving the person(s) involved in each situation.

_____

_____

_____

_____

➢ List three future issues or events you worry about. For each, make a list of the things you can control and the things that you can no longer control and need to surrender. Focus only on what you can control.

_____

_____

_____

_____

➢ For the next day, promise yourself to raise a mental red flag when your mind takes you to the past or future events on your list. Recognize that these thoughts are perfectly normal. When you notice these thoughts, gently turn your attention to the present moment. By becoming more aware, your thoughts will naturally begin to subside.

_____

_____

_____

_____

EXERCISE #4: TRY A FINANCIAL FAST

(Time to complete: 7 to 21 days)

If you spend more than you should, consider a financial fast! Choose a spending ban anywhere from one to three weeks. By doing so, you'll increase your spending awareness and save some cash. During your financial fast, do not use any credit cards, if possible, and do not go to any malls or retail stores. Delete retail apps on your devices and do not purchase any restaurant food or coffee—make everything at home and pay for your groceries in cash. If you need to get a gift for a friend, consider making them something, regifting an item you haven't used, or being honest with them about your cleanse. This exercise will help you become more mindful of excess.

EXERCISE #5: SPEND MINDFULLY

(Time to complete: one week minimum; lifetime practice recommended)

For the next week, at least, keep a log of your spending. Before you spend money, ask yourself:

➤ Is spending money on this item or service absolutely necessary? If not, can I afford it?

_____

_____

_____

_____

➤ Will this expense bring me closer or further away from my personal, professional, and financial goals?

_____

_____

_____

_____

➤ Does this purchase feel aligned with my values?

_____

_____

_____

_____

➤ Do I feel clear about this purchase in my gut?

_____

_____

_____

_____

At the end of the week, write about anything you noticed—such as spending less money because you were more conscious of it.

EXERCISE #6: THE PRESENCE WHEEL

(Time to complete: 20 minutes)

Date: _____

Rate your response after each question using a number from the following scale:

Poor (1-3), Fair (4-5), Good (6-7), Prosperous (8-10)									
Poor			**Fair**			**Good**		**Prosperous**	
1	2	3	4	5	6	7	8	9	10

Connect to Breath: How good are you at regularly drawing attention to your breath and connecting with the here and now; slowing and deepening your breath to reduce stress and promote relaxation?   _____

Body Awareness: How good are you at bringing your attention to the present moment by noticing feelings and sensations in the body?   _____

Daily Mindfulness: Recording your mindfulness practices in an app or journal can keep you on track. How good are you at setting aside at least five minutes a day for stillness, breathwork, meditation, prayer, or yoga?   _____

Mindful Living: How would you rate yourself when it comes to living consciously through mindful eating, environmentally conscious choices, scheduling time for transitions, and not texting while driving?   _____

Distraction Awareness: How good are you at noticing your mind chatter, diversions, and distractions that keep you from being present, and redirecting your attention to the breath and body?   _____

Relationships: How present are you in your personal relationships with friends, family, your partner, and your children—for example, making eye contact and practicing active listening while not being on a device?   _____

Work: When it comes to your work relationships and your attentiveness during meetings or while working on a task or project, how would you rate your ability to be present?   _____

Financial Life: How would you rate yourself when it comes to applying mindfulness to your finances so you spend within your means and don't accrue unnecessary debt?   _____

Single-Tasking: How would you rate yourself when it comes to focusing your attention on the task at hand; eliminating distractions by closing tabs, turning off your phone, or closing your door?　　　　——

Unplug: How good are you at making a conscious effort to take breaks from your devices by using auto response messages, Do Not Disturb mode, or turning off your phone?　　　　——

Connect to Nature: How often do you notice the sky, wind, trees, flowers, and spend time enjoying nature to connect with presence?　　　　——

Intuition: How would you rate yourself when it comes to tuning into your inner compass, connecting with the wisdom of your body and gut instincts, or noticing random thoughts or images that may be intuitive insights?　　　　——

Chart your responses on The Presence Wheel. Start at the top: are you Poor, Prosperous, or somewhere in between when it comes to being able to Connect to Breath? Put a dot on the spoke next to the number that corresponds with your answer. Now continue going around the wheel and after scoring yourself on every spoke, connect the dots to create a circle.

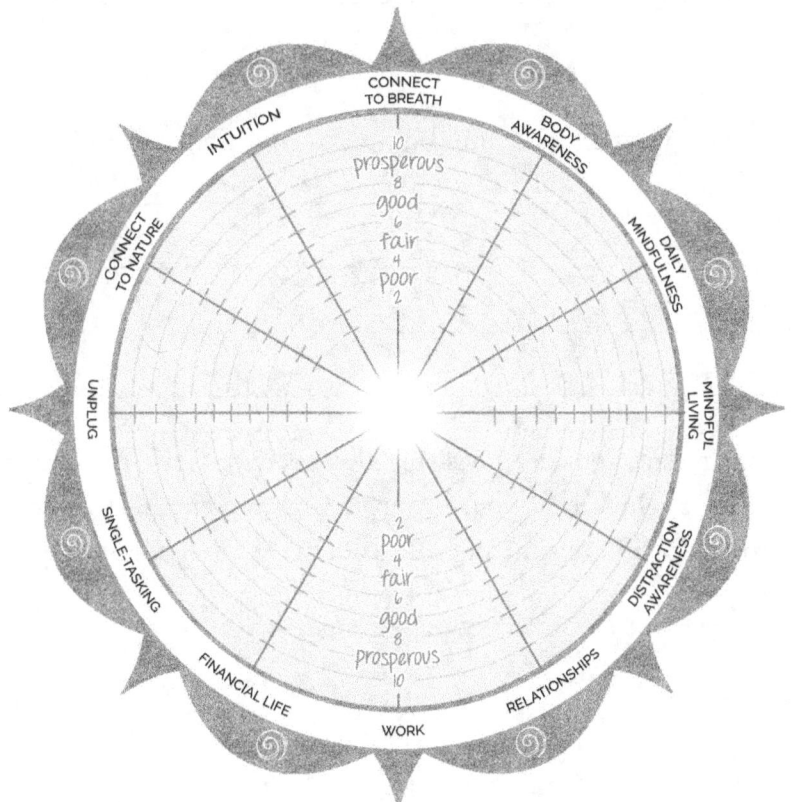

The Presence Wheel

Answer the following questions:

➤ As you look at the three spokes that have the lowest scores (the biggest dents in your wheel), list two ways you can do better right now in these areas

_____

_____

_____

_____

➤ How might you create some accountability for cultivating presence?

_____

_____

_____

_____

➤ What are two new ways to apply mindfulness to your financial life?

_____

_____

_____

_____

To become more present, consider revisiting this exercise weekly or monthly to set yourself up for greater success. Don't beat yourself up if your scores are low—we are all works in progress and have room for improvement. Date your wheel and file it so you can track your progress over time.

CHAPTER - 5

Essence

EXERCISE #1: THERAPY SESSION NUMBER 5

(Time to complete: 20 minutes)

Hello there! In this session you will become aware of how your ego is harming your financial health. You will also learn how connecting with your essence—your inner light—can catapult you into higher heights of success! Let's get started. Please write your responses to the following questions:

➢ What did my "Dear Ego" letter bring up for you in relation to your own ego?

_____

_____

_____

_____

➢ How might your ego be hurting you financially?

_____

_____

_____

_____

_____

➢ In what ways do you connect with your inner light (essence) and let it shine?

_____

_____

_____

_____

➢ How has that connection increased your prosperity? How can you expand on this?

_____

_____

_____

_____

➢ What do you imagine I, as your therapist, might say about what you wrote?

_____

_____

_____

_____

➢ What are two or three insights you gained from this session?

_____

_____

_____

_____

Excellent self-reflection! You will benefit from having taken a deeper look at yourself.

Now, let's give you some tools to continue to detach from your ego and connect with your essence.

EXERCISE #2: ALIGN WITH YOUR ESSENCE

(Time to complete: 20 minutes; lifetime practice)

Answer the following questions to help you get back to your core self:

➢ What values do you hold most deeply?

_____

_____

_____

_____

➢ Do you live in a way that is congruent to these values? In what ways is your life incongruent with these values?

_____

_____

_____

_____

➢ What broad steps might you take to change your life so you can live in a way that is more consistent with your core values?

_____

_____

_____

_____

EXERCISE #3: CANCEL YOUR EGO TRIP

(Time to complete: 20 minutes; lifetime practice)

Answer the following questions:

➤ Which Diva and Doormat characteristics do you recognize in yourself?

_____

_____

_____

_____

➤ When do these characteristics get expressed? How has this hurt you financially?

_____

_____

_____

_____

➤ What will you do to re-center yourself and become your Successful Self with healthy self-esteem?

_____

_____

_____

_____

EXERCISE #4: THE ESSENCE WHEEL

(Time to complete: 20 minutes)

Date: _____

Rate your response after each question using a number from the following scale:

Poor (1-3), Fair (4-5), Good (6-7), Prosperous (8-10)									
Poor			**Fair**			**Good**		**Prosperous**	
1	2	3	4	5	6	7	8	9	10

Essence Alignment: This is about connecting with your deepest self and unique light through presence. How are you aligning your life with essence, this core aspect of self and choosing love over fear? _____

Ego Detachment: This is the ability to observe and separate from harmful aspects of ego such as defensiveness, competition, arrogance, feelings of superiority or inferiority, and focusing on externals, such as appearance and accomplishments. How well are you able to avoid having your financial perspective become distorted by ego? _____

Healthy Self-Esteem: This comes from feeling positive about yourself in relation to others in a balanced way, and includes healthy ego strength, confidence, and assertiveness. How good are you at celebrating your strengths and recognizing your areas of needed growth and development? _____

Humility: Humility involves a healthy awareness of all you do not know or understand, your areas of deficit, and keeping your ego in check. How good are you at remaining humble, modest, and down-to-earth even as you achieve great success? _____

Respect: How would you rate yourself when it comes to demonstrating respect for yourself and others in your communication? _____

Authenticity: How good are you at being honest, real, and genuine with others, while remaining kind and not putting up false pretenses? _____

Vulnerability: Vulnerability is about breaking down the walls created by your ego for self-protection. These walls prevent the honest communication that leads to support, connection, intimacy, and growth. How good are you at admitting what you do not know and asking for help? _____

Enoughness: I define "enoughness" as resisting the urge to feed ego with materialism and staying connected with essence as you welcome true prosperity, which includes generosity. How good are you at knowing that on the essence level, you are always enough?   _____

Use Gifts: How good are you at celebrating your gifts and strengths and aligning them with a need in the world?   _____

Purpose: How would you rate yourself when it comes to identifying your higher personal and professional feeling of purpose, which is fueled by your essence?   _____

Values: How good are you at staying true to yourself and living your life in a way that is aligned with your core values?   _____

Highest Self-Expression: How would you rate yourself when it comes to letting your inner light shine by showing up and thriving in the world as your most expansive, vibrant, and prosperous self?   _____

Chart your responses on The Essence Wheel. Start at the top: are you Poor, Prosperous, or somewhere in between when it comes to Essence Alignment? Put a dot on the spoke next to the number that corresponds with your answer. Now, continue going around the wheel and after scoring yourself on every spoke, connect the dots to create a circle.

ESSENCE ALIGNMENT
EGO DETACHMENT
HEALTHY SELF-ESTEEM
HUMILITY
RESPECT
AUTHENTICITY
VULNERABILITY
ENOUGHNESS
USE GIFTS
PURPOSE
VALUES
HIGHEST SELF EXPRESSION
10
prosperous
8
good
6
fair
4
poor
2
2
poor
4
fair
6
good
8
prosperous
10

The Essence Wheel

Let's wrap this up by answering the following questions:

- Look at the three spokes of The Essence Wheel with the lowest scores (the dents) and come up with two ways you can improve in each of those areas.

____

____

_____

_____

➤ What are two ways detaching from ego and aligning with essence would improve your financial life?

_____

_____

_____

_____

➤ How can you spend more of your time in the healthy self-esteem range?

_____

_____

_____

_____

No matter what your results are, consider revisiting this exercise monthly or quarterly to continue to keep your ego in check and ignite success by connecting with essence. Date your wheel and file it for later reference!

CHAPTER - 6

Self-Love

EXERCISE #1: THERAPY SESSION NUMBER 6

(Time to complete: 20 minutes)

This session will help you feel so much better! Today, you will become aware of your Inner Saboteur and start loving yourself the way you deserve. Answer the following questions:

➤ How has your Inner Saboteur prevented you from greater happiness and prosperity?

_____

_____

_____

_____

➤ What did my story bring up for you and how does this relate to your own self-love?

_____

_____

_____

_____

➢ How might your life look different if you embraced yourself with fierce love?

_____

_____

_____

_____

What do you think about what you just wrote? Does your relationship with yourself leave some room for improvement? Never fear! I'm here to help!

EXERCISE #2: FACE YOUR INNER SABOTEUR

(Time to complete: 10 minutes a day for one week minimum; lifetime practice)

Give your Inner Saboteur (iSab) a name and then visualize or even draw what your iSab looks like (this adds to the fun!). For a week, write how your iSab impacts you. On the last day, review your entries and respond to the following questions:

➤ What did your iSab like to pester you about?

_____

_____

_____

_____

➤ Did you notice any trends around the circumstances or timing of when your iSab tends to appear?

_____

_____

_____

_____

➤ On a scale from 1 to 10, how badly do you think your iSab is hurting your mental health? Physical health? Financial health?

_____

_____

_____

_____

Now, close your eyes and imagine you are telling your iSab to quiet down. What happened when you attempted to do that? If you weren't able to quell your inner villain, have no fear. Your Inner Dream Team is here!

EXERCISE #3: CULTIVATE YOUR INNER DREAM TEAM

(Time to complete: 15 minutes; lifetime practice)

Rate how your Inner Dream Team members are performing on a scale from 1 to 10, with 1 being not at all supportive and 10 being fully supportive:

Positive Coach (self-affirmation) ____

- Best Friend (self-compassion) ____

- Loving Parent (self-care) ____

- Once you've determined the role with the lowest score, answer the following questions:

➤ Why is this aspect of inner support most challenging for you?

_____

_____

_____

_____

➤ How can you increase your performance in this role?

_____

_____

_____

_____

For the next day or two, imagine that this Inner Dream Team member is right alongside you. Try to hear their voice and what they might say to support you. Then, answer the following questions:

➤ Do you notice any benefits? For example, does your Inner Dream Team member motivate you or help you feel better?

_____

_____

_____

_____

➤ With the help of your Inner Dream Team, did you notice a decrease in the influence of your iSab and the negative emotions it triggers?

_____

_____

_____

Remember to call upon your Inner Dream Team members whenever you need them!

EXERCISE #4: THE SELF-LOVE WHEEL

(Time to complete: 20 minutes)

Date: _____

Rate your response after each question using a number from the following scale:

Poor (1-3), Fair (4-5), Good (6-7), Prosperous (8-10)									
Poor			Fair			Good		Prosperous	
1	2	3	4	5	6	7	8	9	10

Self-Compassion: Self-compassion is the ability to silence your inner saboteur, practice self-forgiveness and self-acceptance, and be your most compassionate advocate. It is the opposite of self-flagellation or excessive guilt and regret—it is a mental state where you recognize mistakes, learn from them, and get back on track. How would you rate yourself when it comes to self-compassion? _____

Self-Affirmation: How would you rate yourself when it comes to honoring your strengths, gifts, and unique abilities and seeing all that is beautiful and good about you? _____

Grow & Learn: When it comes to investing in activities, classes, and independent learning to help you grow and develop, how would you rate yourself? _____

Nutrition: Healthy eating includes limiting sugar and processed foods, cooking at home, eating balanced meals, taking multivitamins, and portion control. How would you rate yourself when it comes to nutrition? _____

Hydrate: Skipping the soda and energy drinks and drinking enough water is important for good health. How good are you when it comes to hydration? _____

Physical Activity: When it comes to physical activity, how would you rate yourself? _____

Appearance: How would you rate yourself when it comes to grooming yourself with love and care and putting yourself together so that you feel like the beautiful person that you are?

_____

Health Care: This includes annual physicals, dental care, mental health counseling, and specialty care or holistic care as needed. What's your priority when it comes to your own health care? _____

Moderate Substance Use: How would you rate yourself when it comes to moderating caffeine, alcohol, sleep aids, or other substances in your life?   _____

Solitude/Reflection: This is stillness and quiet time when you can connect with yourself. How good are you at prioritizing time for solitude and reflection?   _____

Connect to Nature: This includes connecting with the outdoors, animals, or plants. How would you rate your ability to connect with nature?   _____

Sleep: Making sure you get enough sleep and have the ability to fall asleep easily and stay asleep is also important for good health. How would you rate yourself when it comes to prioritizing your sleep?   _____

Leisure/Hobbies: It's important to relax and enjoy activities such as art, music, or sports. How would you rate yourself when it comes to making time for leisure and hobbies?   _____

Manage Time: Time management is all about setting healthy time boundaries between your work and your personal life. Make sure to unplug from technology—turn off your phone before bedtime and during mealtimes, do not respond to work emails after work hours or while on vacation, and limit screen time. How would you rate yourself when it comes to striking a nice balance in terms of connecting with others and allowing time for solitude?   _____

Home Environment: Keeping your home clean, organized, and functional is important when establishing a pleasant sanctuary for yourself. How would you rate your home environment?

_____

Tend to Finances: Making sure there is a healthy balance between the flow of saving and spending, and treating yourself within your means is very important. How would you rate yourself when it comes to taking care of your financial life?   _____

Chart your responses on The Self-Love Wheel. Start at the top: are you Poor, Prosperous, or somewhere in between when it comes to Self-Compassion? Put a dot on the spoke next to the number that corresponds with your answer. Now, continue going around the wheel and after scoring yourself on every spoke, connect the dots to create a circle.

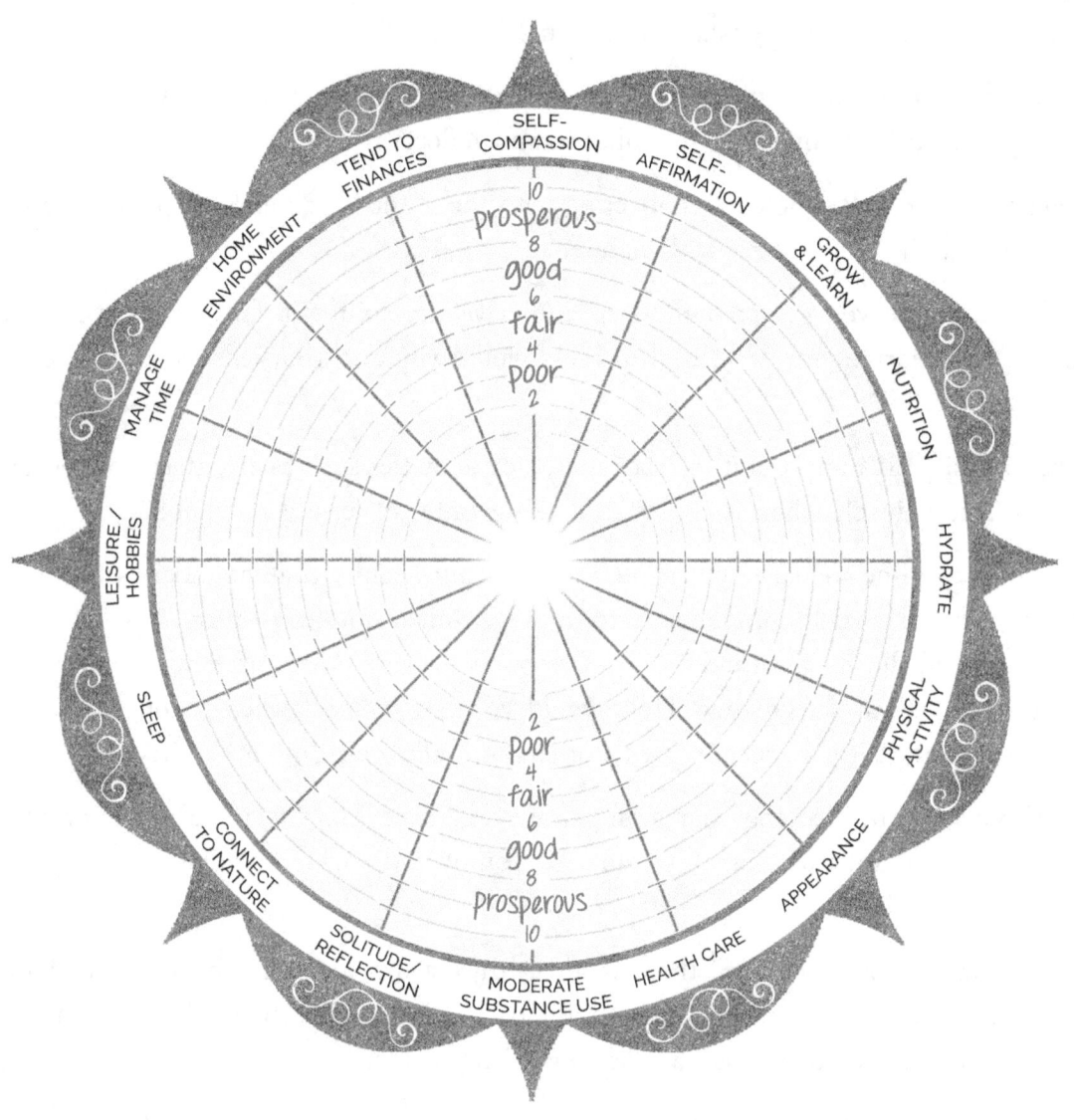

The Self-Love Wheel

Don't worry if you didn't score as well as you hoped. That just means you can look for opportunities to do better when it comes to loving yourself. Answer the following questions:

> As you review your wheel, identify the three spokes with the lowest scores (the biggest dents) and list two ways you can do better right now for each spoke.

_____

_____

_____

_____

➤ How might you create some accountability for increasing your self-love?

_____

_____

_____

_____

➤ What are two ways to improve your financial self-care?

_____

_____

_____

_____

Consider revisiting this exercise weekly or monthly to continue to cultivate self-love and to welcome greater prosperity. Don't forget to date your wheel and file it for later reference so you can track your progress over time.

CHAPTER -

Vision

EXERCISE #1: THERAPY SESSION NUMBER 7

(Time to complete: 20 minutes)

Welcome back to my office. Today, we are going to look at your life's vision or plan. Use this session to write a letter to yourself where you envision your best life, just as I did while going through my divorce. Act as if you are already living your best life and share what that looks like. To get started, ask yourself:

➢ In that best life, how would you spend your time at work?

_____

_____

_____

_____

➢ In that best life, how would you spend your time away from work? Include details about your family, social life, and hobbies that you enjoy.

_____

_____

_____

_____

➤ Write your letter below:

_____

_____

_____

_____

Now, read through your letter and take note of any common themes. It's time to make your vision a reality.

EXERCISE #2: DECLARE A PERSONAL MANIFESTO

(Time to complete: 10 minutes)

A Personal Manifesto is a declaration of your core values, what you stand for, and how you intend to live your life. It provides a foundation to build or rebuild your life, motivates you to live more fully, and reminds you to stay on course even during challenging times.

My Personal Manifesto is: "I live with loving compassion, fearless courage, and vibrant joy. I share myself in everything I do with the highest intention to provide inspiration and support to ease suffering and promote connection and growth. I live a supported, balanced, joyful, and prosperous life."

Experts provide best practices for writing a manifesto. As you prepare to write your manifesto, ask yourself:

➤ What are my unique gifts and strengths?

_____

_____

_____

_____

➤ What are my strongest beliefs and values?

_____

_____

_____

_____

➤ How do I want to live my life?

_____

_____

_____

_____

_____

➤ What do I most enjoy? What do I find most meaningful and rewarding?

_____

_____

_____

_____

➤ What changes do I need to make to live my best life?

_____

_____

_____

_____

Now give it a go! In three to five sentences, declare the highest intention for your life. Keep it positive and write in the present tense with confident language. Include aspects of your personal, professional, and financial life. Consider hanging your manifesto on your fridge or corkboard, or use it as your screensaver.

EXERCISE #3: DREAM BIG DREAMS

(Time to complete: 30 minutes; lifetime practice)

Answer the following questions:

➤ If you had a magic wand, what would your life look like? What are your dreams and ambitions? Include personal, professional, and financial aspirations.

_____

_____

_____

_____

➤ What's on your bucket list? Write five to ten things you would like to experience, including travel goals.

_____

_____

_____

_____

➤ Finally, what do you want your legacy to be? What positive mark do you want to leave on the world? What are your philanthropy goals?

_____

_____

_____

Now, here's the kicker, I want you to tell somebody about what you wrote. This makes it real and puts it out into the universe as a formal request. While this can be uncomfortable, especially when you think you are asking for too much, remember that you aren't! Telling a loved one or a trusted confidant is a critical step toward committing to your vision.

EXERCISE #4: DEVELOP AN ACTION PLAN

(Time to complete: 45 minutes; lifetime practice)

Developing an action plan for your personal, professional, and financial vision can seem overwhelming, but it doesn't have to be complicated or time consuming, in fact, it's best to keep it simple. Just follow these instructions:

➤ Write four to six personal, professional, and financial goals for the next year and then rank them in order of importance. Make sure to include at least two financial goals.

_____

_____

_____

_____

➤ Make sure they are Specific, Measurable, Achievable, Realistic, and Timely (SMART) goals. For example, "Invest $15,000 in my retirement fund this year" versus "Save a gazillion dollars before I am ninety-nine."

_____

_____

_____

_____

➤ Break goals down into smaller objectives or tasks, such as calling your financial advisor within the next week to share your goals so they can help put together a plan to help you get there or set up automatic monthly payments of $1,250.

_____

_____

_____

_____

➤ Create some accountability by sharing your goals, especially with your financial planner and/or therapist, and scheduling regular follow-ups to keep you on track.

_____

_____

_____

_____

By completing this exercise, you are gaining traction on your vision, congratulations!

EXERCISE #5: LIVE WITH INTENTION

(Time to complete: 10 minutes; lifetime practice)

An intention is a way of being or living, stated in the present, that supports the likelihood of your goals coming to fruition. Wayne Dyer, author of *The Power of Intention*, said, "Our intentions create our reality."

Okay, let's do this.

➤ On separate pages, write down your personal, professional, and financial intentions. Your financial intention may be, "I am not wasteful and spend wisely."

➤ On each page, write three to five short and positive intentions that support you in achieving your goals.

➤ Consider reviewing or reciting your intentions before your daily morning or nighttime meditations. The more you repeat them the more likely they are to come true.

➤ Create daily practices to support your intentions. In the yogic tradition, the term *sadhana* refers to the daily practices that are a means for accomplishing something. Yogi Jaggi Vasudev, also known as Sadhguru, says, "Everything can be sadhana. The way you eat, the way you sit, the way you stand, the way you breathe, the way you conduct your body, mind and your energies and emotions—this is sadhana. Sadhana does not mean any specific kind of activity, sadhana means you are using everything as a tool for your well-being." Make your intentions your way of life.

EXERCISE #6: VISUALIZE SUCCESS

(Time to complete: 15 minutes; lifetime practice)

Visualizing a positive outcome has long been utilized in sports psychology—if you can envision yourself making the goal, the chances are more likely that you will. Many neuroscientists have found that visualization helps the body respond better in its pursuit of desired outcomes, including financial goals like saving and accumulating wealth. That's why bank managers and financial consultants should set clear goals that are easy for clients to visualize. It can motivate them to maximize their effort and performance so they can maximize their savings.

To reduce nervousness, give me more confidence, and improve my performance, I envision my speaking engagements and media appearances going well. Now, it's time for you to give positive visualization a try. With your eyes closed, pretend you already achieved your life's vision. Envision your greatest life filled with prosperity, love, health, support, success, and anything you desire. This includes your personal and professional life. How does it feel to achieve your life vision?

EXERCISE #7: THE VISION WHEEL

(Time to complete: 20 minutes)

Date: _____

Rate your response after each question using a number from the following scale:

Poor (1-3), Fair (4-5), Good (6-7), Prosperous (8-10)									
Poor			**Fair**			**Good**		**Prosperous**	
1	2	3	4	5	6	7	8	9	10

Life Plan: A life plan is an overarching life vision that includes a Personal Manifesto by which you live. How well are you doing at creating a life plan? _____

Professional Plan: This is a career or business plan that will help you align your gifts with a need in the world. How would you rate yourself at coming up with a professional plan?

_____

Work-Life Balance: A work-life balance plan protects your personal life, including your relationships and overall well-being. When it comes to work-life balance, how would you rate your ability to come up with a plan? _____

Financial Plan: This spoke refers to the Financial Planning component on The Financial Health Wheel you completed in the introduction. How would you rate yourself when it comes to creating a financial plan with goals, action items, and accountability? _____

Intentional Living: Living with intention is living according to positive statements that reflect ways of being that will help you achieve your goals and vision. How would you rate yourself when it comes to living with intention? _____

Visualize Success: This is the practice of regularly envisioning yourself achieving success in various aspects of your life. How good are you at visualizing success in all aspects of your life?

_____

Daily Practices: Having daily personal, professional, and/or financial behaviors or routines will help you achieve your vision. How well do your daily practices help support your vision?

_____

Health Goals: Your mental, physical, and spiritual wellness and aspirations are your health goals. How well do your health goals apply to your overall well-being? _____

Relationship Goals: These are your needs and ideals for love, connection, and support aspirations. How much thought have you put into what you want your relationships to look like?

_____

Fulfill Hobbies: Do you take time for fun and leisure activities that you enjoy? How much priority do your hobbies have in your life? _____

Philanthropy Plan: Do you have a plan for how you are going to be of service to the world in a greater way; are you clear on the legacy you want to leave behind? How would you rate yourself when it comes to creating a philanthropy plan? _____

Bucket List: This is a list of experiences that you want to be sure to get out of life. How good have you been at identifying what you want on your bucket list? _____

Chart your responses on The Vision Wheel. Start at the top: are you Poor, Prosperous, or somewhere in between when it comes to having an overarching Life Plan? Put a dot on the spoke next to the number that corresponds with your answer. Now, continue going around the wheel and after scoring yourself on every spoke, connect the dots to create a circle. Remember, you are measuring if you have created a plan for that vision, not if you've achieved that vision. That will come in time!

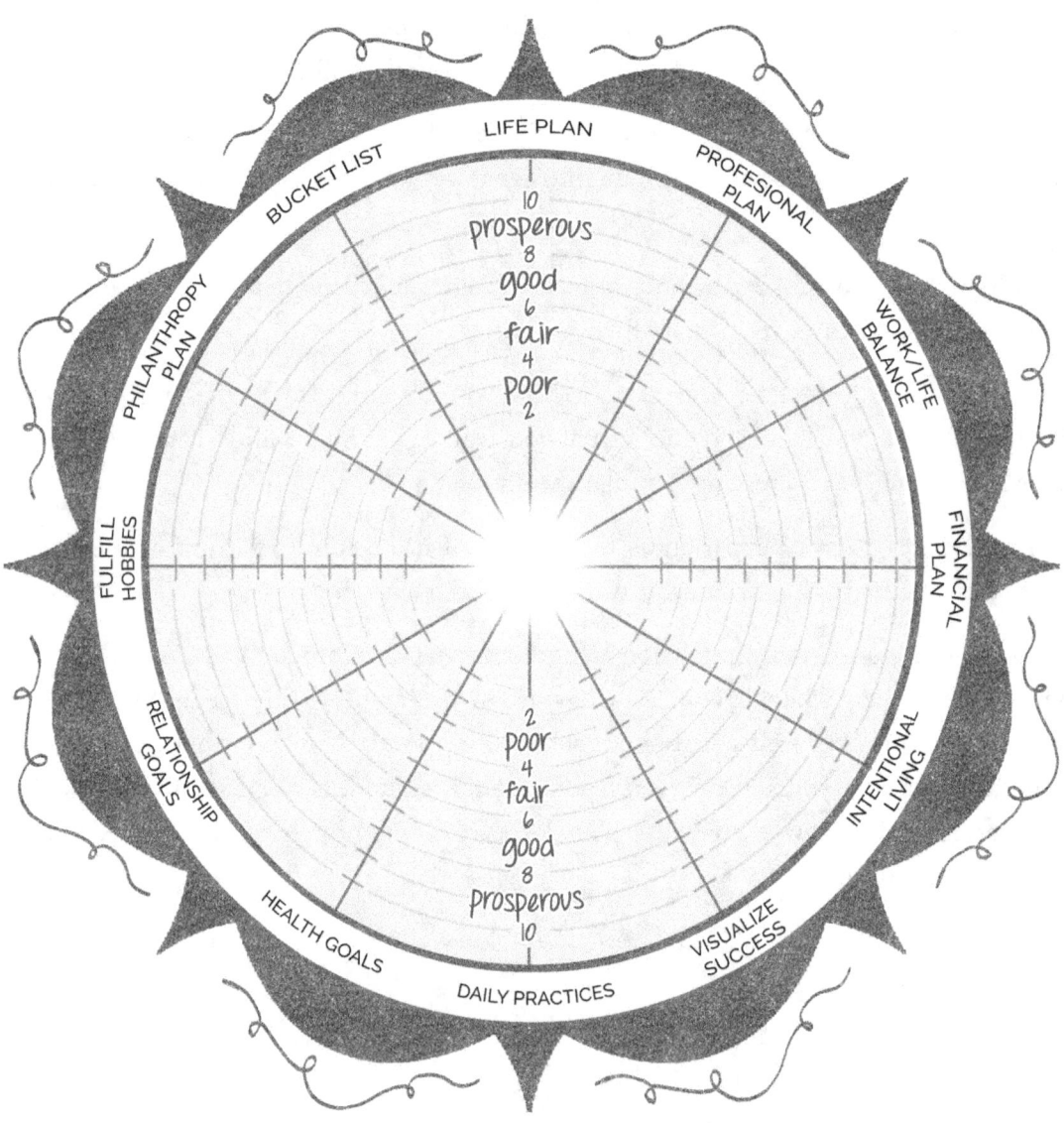

The Vision Wheel

Answer the following questions:

➤ As you look at the biggest dents in The Vision Wheel, what areas are in most need of attention when it comes to creating a vision?

_____

_____

> What roadblocks or challenges are you experiencing when it comes to improving your vision in certain areas?

_____

_____

_____

_____

> What kind of support do you need?

_____

_____

_____

_____

> Consider revisiting this exercise quarterly to continue to clarify your vision of a full and abundant life. Date your wheel and file it for later reference so you can track your progress over time.

_____

_____

_____

_____

CHAPTER - **8**

Support

EXERCISE #1: THERAPY SESSION NUMBER 8

(Time to complete: 20 minutes)

Hello again! Today we are going to help you welcome more support in your life. Answer the following questions:

➤ Name two major challenges you have had in your life. Who helped you get through these challenges and how did they help?

_____

_____

_____

_____

➤ What four people have been most instrumental in supporting you in achieving your personal and professional vision? How did their input change your life's trajectory?

_____

_____

_____

_____

➤ Do you have a mentor who helps guide your career? How have they helped you achieve success?

_____

_____

_____

_____

➤ Where in your life could you use some additional support?

_____

_____

_____

_____

➤ Think back to your life vision from the previous chapter. If you could add anyone to your support team, who would it be and how would they help you achieve your vision?

_____

_____

_____

_____

EXERCISE #2: REPLENISH YOURSELF

(Time to complete: 15 minutes; lifetime practice)

Answer the following questions:

➢ If your support network was a bank account, would you have a positive balance or be overdrawn? Why is this?

_____

_____

_____

_____

➢ Do you routinely give more than you receive? If so, how can you better replenish yourself by receiving support?

_____

_____

_____

_____

➢ What would your life look like if you had a healthy balance of giving and receiving support? How can you make this happen?

_____

_____

_____

_____

EXERCISE #3: REMOVE BARRIERS TO RECEIVING SUPPORT

(Time to complete: 25 minutes; lifetime practice)

Answer the following questions:

➤ Which three to five barriers do you feel are your biggest obstacles to receiving support?

_____

_____

_____

_____

➤ In what ways do these barriers negatively impact your life?

_____

_____

_____

_____

➤ What are three ways to transcend these barriers this week?

_____

_____

_____

_____

Wonderful! In the next week, ask for support three times when you normally would not. Write about how it felt. It's okay if some of the feelings were uncomfortable, as seeking support is a skill that takes practice and needs to be developed.

EXERCISE #4: THE SUPPORT NETWORK WHEEL

(Time to complete: 20 minutes)

Date: _____

Rate your response after each question using a number from the following scale:

Poor (1-3), Fair (4-5), Good (6-7), Prosperous (8-10)									
Poor			**Fair**			**Good**		**Prosperous**	
1	2	3	4	5	6	7	8	9	10

Physical Health: Those who help you take care of your physical health include your primary doctor, specialty doctors, holistic health providers, dentist, eye doctor, healer, massage therapist, nutritionist, personal trainer, physical therapist, and workout buddy. When it comes to having the right support system to take care of your physical health, how would you rate yourself?

_____

Mental Health: Those who help promote your mental health include your therapist and psychiatrist, your significant other, family, life coach, support groups, and 12-step sponsor. When it comes to your mental health, how is your support system looking? _____

Emotional: Those who provide you with emotional support might include your partner, family, and friends. How would you rate yourself when it comes to having the right emotional support? _____

Career: People who provide professional support include your career counselor or coach, consultant, mentor, peers in professional associations, and your supervisor. If you are a student, this support team would include academic advisors, teachers, and supportive classmates. If you are a stay-at-home parent, this would include people who support you in your parenting community. How would you rate yourself when it comes to having a support system for your career? _____

Financial: People who help keep you on track financially can include your accountant, asset manager, a debt consolidation service, support group, estate planning attorney, accountability partner, or financial planner. You might also list organizations or people who help you out financially through loans, grants, loan forgiveness, or other financial assistance. How supported do you feel when it comes to your financial life? _____

Joyce Marter, LCPC, CSP®

Family Connection: This includes your parents, siblings, children, chosen family, extended family, your partner's family, and your pets. How would you rate your family support system?

_____

Friendship: For this section, think of meaningful friends who serve as trusted confidants and provide comradery, companionship, loyalty, care, and fun. When it comes to supportive friends, how would you rate your network?

_____

Partnership: If you have a significant other, list them here. If you are dating or romantically involved with more than one person, you can list them all here. If you don't have a significant other and don't want one, rate yourself a 10 instead of answering the question. If you are in a partnership, how would you rate the support you receive?

_____

Social/Community: These are groups or events that provide social support and could include your place of worship, community events, concerts, gatherings with friends, gym, meditation groups, membership in organizations, your neighborhood, prayer group, 12-step group, yoga studio, parenting group, or online support system. How well are you utilizing the support that you could receive from your community?

_____

Hobbies: This section is for the people who support you in doing your hobbies, including your band members, a tennis partner, an intramural sports team, a running group, an art studio, or a gaming group. How well are you doing when it comes to receiving support from people who participate in your favorite hobbies?

_____

Logistics Helpers: By logistics helpers, I mean people or services that help you with the tasks related to daily living. For example, your roommate, partner, kids, neighbors, or babysitting co-op. Include people or services you hire, such as a childcare provider, dog walker, housekeeper, lawn service, grocery delivery, meal prep service, and so forth. How would you rate yourself when it comes to asking for support with specific daily tasks? _____

Spiritual: List those who provide you with spiritual support including God or your Higher Power, your priest/rabbi/pastor/spiritual advisor, meditation coach, psychic/medium, yogi, energy healer, shaman, soul coach, or other. When it comes to your spirituality, how would you rate yourself when it comes to asking for support?

_____

Chart your numbered responses and then connect the dots. Start at the top: are you Poor, Prosperous, or somewhere in between when it comes to having a support network to boost your Physical Health? Put a dot on the spoke next to the number that corresponds with your answer. Continue going around the wheel, and after scoring yourself on every spoke, connect the dots to create a circle.

The Support Network Wheel

Now, at the end of each spoke, list the names or titles of people or organizations that provide you with this type of support. It's okay to list the same person, title, or organization in more than one spoke.

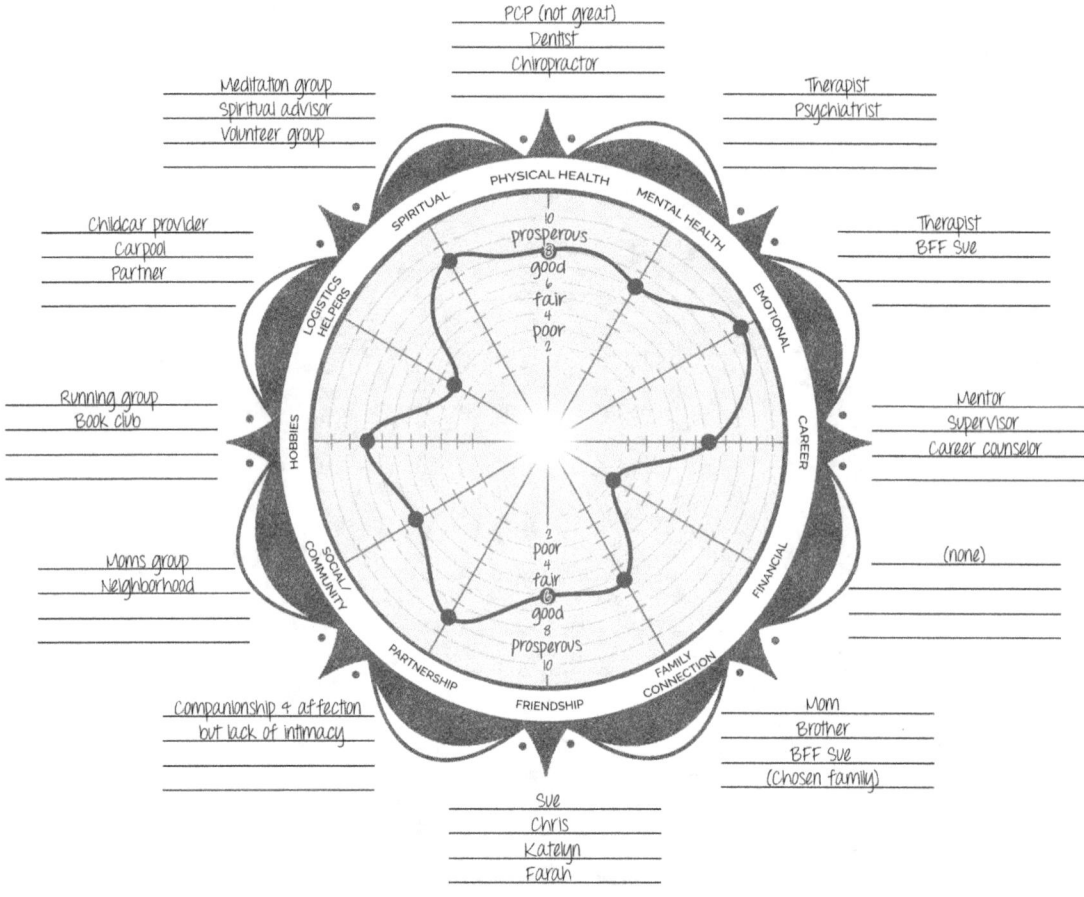

PCP (not great)
Dentist
Chiropractor

Meditation group
Spiritual advisor
Volunteer group

Therapist
Psychiatrist

Childcar provider
Carpool
Partner

Therapist
BFF Sue

Running group
Book club

Mentor
Supervisor
Career counselor

Moms group
Neighborhood

(none)

Companionship & affection
but lack of intimacy

Mom
Brother
BFF Sue
(chosen family)

Sue
Chris
Katelyn
Farah

The Support Network Wheel Example

In this support wheel example, notice the two deepest dents in the wheel in the areas of Financial and Logistics Helpers. Also, notice how few people have been identified to help with these areas.

Now, answer the following questions:

➤ Have you listed anyone in more than one area of support?

_____

_____

_____

_____

➤ This can be wonderful, but make sure you don't rely too heavily on one person. A client listed her husband in almost every area and didn't have too many other people in her close network. This exercise helped her realize that not having more friends or supporters was putting a strain on her relationship with her spouse.

_____

_____

_____

_____

➤ As you look at the dents in your wheel, are there sections where you have little or no support? Another client only had support in the career area, which helped to explain her workaholism.

_____

_____

_____

_____

➤ What three actions can you take to find more support in the areas where you are lacking (the biggest dents)?

_____

_____

_____

_____

Revisit this exercise quarterly to continue assessing your support network. Because support is reciprocal, consider completing this wheel a second time and focusing on the support you give others. This may provide insight into why your balance of give and take might not be optimal just yet.

EXERCISE #5: THE SUPPORT WHEEL

(Time to complete: 20 minutes)

Date: _____

Rate your response after each question using a number from the following scale:

Poor (1-3), Fair (4-5), Good (6-7), Prosperous (8-10)									
Poor			Fair			Good		Prosperous	
1	2	3	4	5	6	7	8	9	10

Plant Seeds: By planting seeds, I mean developing new connections through social activities, community events, professional networking, social media and online outreach, and marketing efforts such as e-blasts, newsletters, or mailings. When it comes to making new connections, how would you rate yourself? _____

Nurture Relationships: How would you rate yourself when it comes to regularly letting people know they are special to you? _____

End Toxic Relationships: By ending and "weeding out" toxic relationships you can empower yourself to set healthy boundaries in relationships you can't choose (like your sister or your boss) and terminate relationships that are truly unhealthy for you. How would you rate yourself when it comes to weeding out toxic relationships? _____

Ask for Help: How good are you at routinely asking for help with tasks as needed and as appropriate? _____

Seek Counsel: When it comes to regularly seeking advice, consultation, or wise counsel from people who are more knowledgeable or experienced in certain areas, how would you rate yourself? _____

Seek Care: How good are you at asking for support when it comes to your mental and physical health, including asking for affection? _____

Balance Giving & Receiving: How good are you at making sure you are striking a healthy balance between being supported and offering support to others? _____

Mentoring: This includes receiving support from others who have achieved what you would like to achieve, and remembering to mentor others when appropriate. How good are you at asking for support from those you admire and then, on the flip side, giving that support to others? _____

Reciprocal Relationships: Reciprocating means striking a healthy balance of independence and dependence in your relationships so that you can experience the benefits of interdependence, including mutuality. How would you rate yourself at forming reciprocal relationships? _____

Permeable Boundaries: How would you rate yourself in ensuring that your emotional and relational boundaries are not too rigid or too loose so you can foster intimacy and connection?

_____

Openly Receiving: When you are feeling the barriers of fear, shame, guilt, or pride, how open are you to receiving support? _____

Financial Support: This includes seeking help from a financial advisor or business consultant and applying for grants, loans, scholarships, loan forgiveness, and financial assistance programs that would support you. How well are you doing with asking and receiving financial support?

_____

Chart your responses on The Support Wheel. Start at the top: are you Poor, Prosperous, or somewhere in between when it comes to being able to Plant Seeds for new relationships? Put a dot on the spoke next to the number that corresponds with your answer. Now, continue going around the wheel and after scoring yourself on every spoke, connect the dots to create a circle.

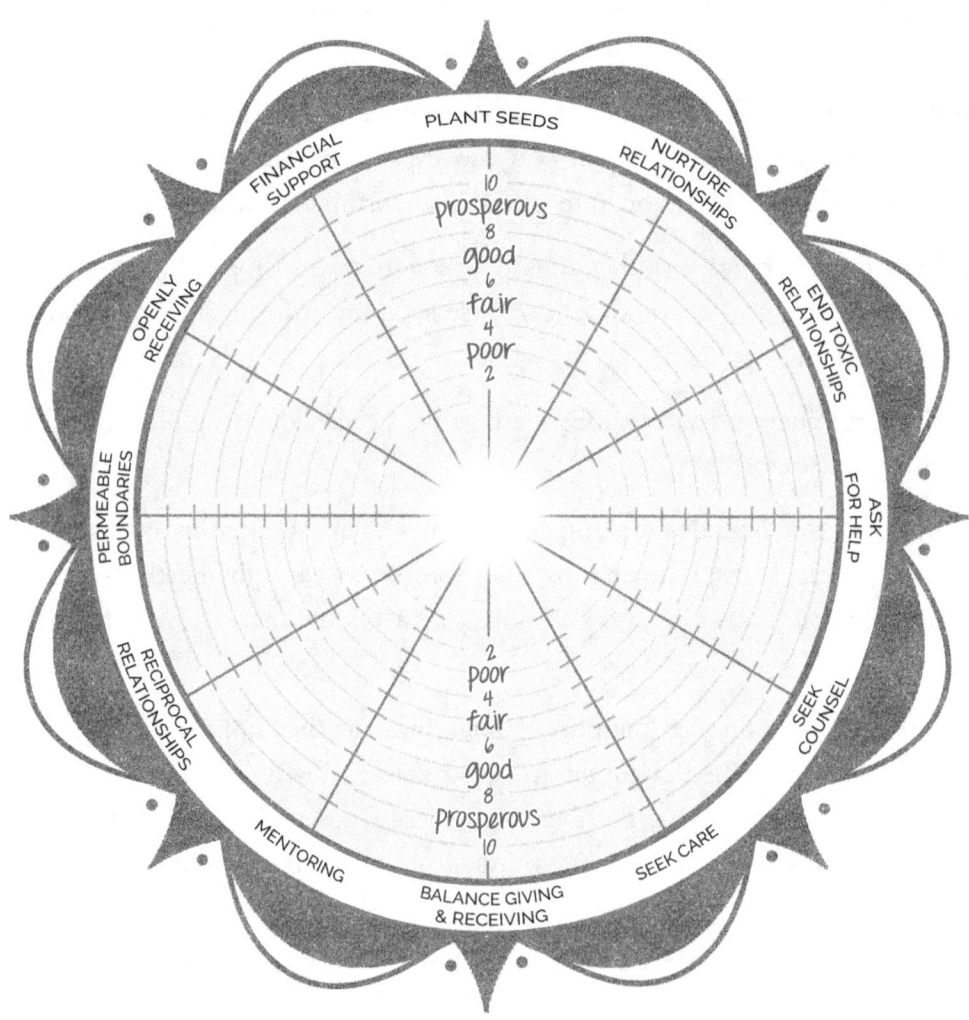

The Support Wheel

Don't worry if you scored poorly on this mindset. Asking for help is often one of the hardest things to do. Keep working on this mindset to see improvements.

Now, answer the following questions:

➢ As you look at the biggest dents in your wheel, do you know why you scored lowest in these areas?

_____

_____

_____

_____

➤ What three action steps can you take to improve in each area?

_____

_____

_____

_____

Date your wheel and file it for later reference. Consider revisiting this exercise monthly or quarterly to continue to create more support in your life. You are on your way to a more supported life. Bravo!

CHAPTER - 9

Compassion

EXERCISE #1: THERAPY SESSION NUMBER 9

(Time to complete: 20 minutes)

Welcome! In today's session, take some time to write about the following:

➤ Recall a time when you felt somebody was compassionate toward you. Maybe they were kind, thoughtful, or empathetic. How did that feel? Did their response change your situation?

_____

_____

_____

_____

➤ Recall an instance when you demonstrated compassion to somebody personally. How about professionally? Write about how this felt.

_____

_____

_____

_____

➤ Consider how demonstrating more compassion might improve your relationships at work and even your finances. Write a best-case scenario describing how this could play out.

_____

_____

_____

_____

➤ What's something you could do today to be more compassionate to the people in your life?

_____

_____

_____

_____

All this good karma will boomerang back at you, leading to true prosperity.

EXERCISE #2: INCREASE SUCCESS THROUGH EMPATHY

(Time to complete: 15 minutes; lifetime practice)

Answer the following questions:

> What opportunities are there to show more empathy in your relationships? Scan through the list of non-empathetic and empathic responses and write down any ideas on what you can say to be more empathetic.

_____

_____

_____

_____

> In what ways can you use nonverbal communication or active listening to express greater empathy?

_____

_____

_____

_____

> What might be the benefit of being more empathetic in a relationship you want to strengthen? How would this improved relationship improve your life?

_____

_____

_____

_____

EXERCISE #3: EXPAND WITH COMPASSION

(Time to complete: 10 minutes; lifetime practice)

Respond to the following questions:

➢ Reflect on a time in which you learned from a relationship or friendship with someone from a different background than you. What did you learn from this experience?

_____

_____

_____

_____

➢ When have you experienced a compassionate connection with somebody and how did that feel? How did it promote positive change in your life?

_____

_____

_____

_____

➢ How can you use what you've learned from these experiences to improve your relationships? How might this expand your life and success?

_____

_____

_____

_____

EXERCISE #4: WIELD THE POWER OF LOVINGKINDNESS

(Time to complete: 15 minutes, lifetime practice)

Answer the following:

➤ Choose a personal relationship you would like to strengthen. This could be a family member, your partner, or a close friend. Why is this person important to you?

_____

_____

_____

_____

➤ List ten attributes you like about this person.

_____

_____

_____

_____

➤ Circle three of these attributes and then find a way to communicate them to the person in the coming week. Notice the effects on your relationship and well-being.

_____

_____

_____

_____

EXERCISE #5: PAY IT FORWARD

(Time to complete: 15 minutes, lifetime practice)

Answer the following questions:

➤ How are you already being of service, altruistic, and/or charitable? How has this improved your mental health?

_____

_____

_____

_____

➤ What keeps you from offering greater generosity in these areas? What needs to happen in order for you to expand your generosity?

_____

_____

_____

_____

➤ How might paying it forward also lead to true prosperity?

_____

_____

_____

_____

EXERCISE #6: THE COMPASSION WHEEL

(Time to complete: 20 minutes)

Date: _____

Rate your response after each question using a number from the following scale:

Poor (1-3), Fair (4-5), Good (6-7), Prosperous (8-10)									
Poor			**Fair**			**Good**		**Prosperous**	
1	2	3	4	5	6	7	8	9	10

Active Listening: Being fully present to the person speaking to you, listening with all your awareness, making sure you clearly understand their message, responding thoughtfully, and remembering what has been said. How would you rate yourself when it comes to active listening? _____

Empathy: Understanding somebody's perspective and what they are feeling, sharing that feeling, and having a desire to help them, if needed. When it comes to having empathy toward others, how would you rate yourself? _____

Kindness: How would you rate yourself when it comes to being friendly, warm, considerate, and thoughtful of others? _____

Encourage: Lifting others up by having faith and confidence in them and fostering hope is encouragement. How good are you at encouraging others? _____

Patience: Being gentle and understanding with others when they may be causing you some delay or inconvenience. How would you rate yourself when it comes to patience? _____

Generosity: Giving more than is required or expected in terms of time, information, assistance, services, money, or other resources. How generous are you? _____

Altruism: When it comes to selfless concern and devotion to the well-being of others, how would you rate yourself? _____

Open-Minded: When it comes to being open to different perspectives, thoughts, behaviors, and ideas without placing judgement, how would you rate yourself? _____

Accept Others: Multicultural awareness, acceptance, and affirmation. This includes acceptance of people from various races, cultures, ethnicities, religions, socioeconomic statuses, political orientation, sexual orientation, gender identity, and lifestyle. How would you rate yourself when it comes to accepting others? _____

Ethics: Upholding sound moral principles that govern your behavior both personally and professionally. Having mercy instead of displaying vengeance or litigiousness. How would you rate yourself when it comes to ethics? _____

Service: Being of service to a person, group, community, or cause through helpful behaviors, volunteer work, leadership, and other acts of contribution. When it comes to being of service to others, how would you rate yourself? _____

Charity: Note that this spoke refers to the Charity component on The Financial Health Wheel that you completed in the introduction. How would you rate yourself when it comes to donating money, food, or other resources to those in need? _____

Chart your responses on The Compassion Wheel. Let's start at the top: are you Poor, Prosperous, or somewhere in between when it comes to Active Listening? Put a dot on the spoke next to the number that corresponds with your answer. Now, continue going around the wheel and after scoring yourself on every spoke, connect the dots to create a circle. If you are having difficulty being honest with your responses, ask a trusted confidant to help you or imagine somebody close to you completing the wheel as if they were answering the questions about you.

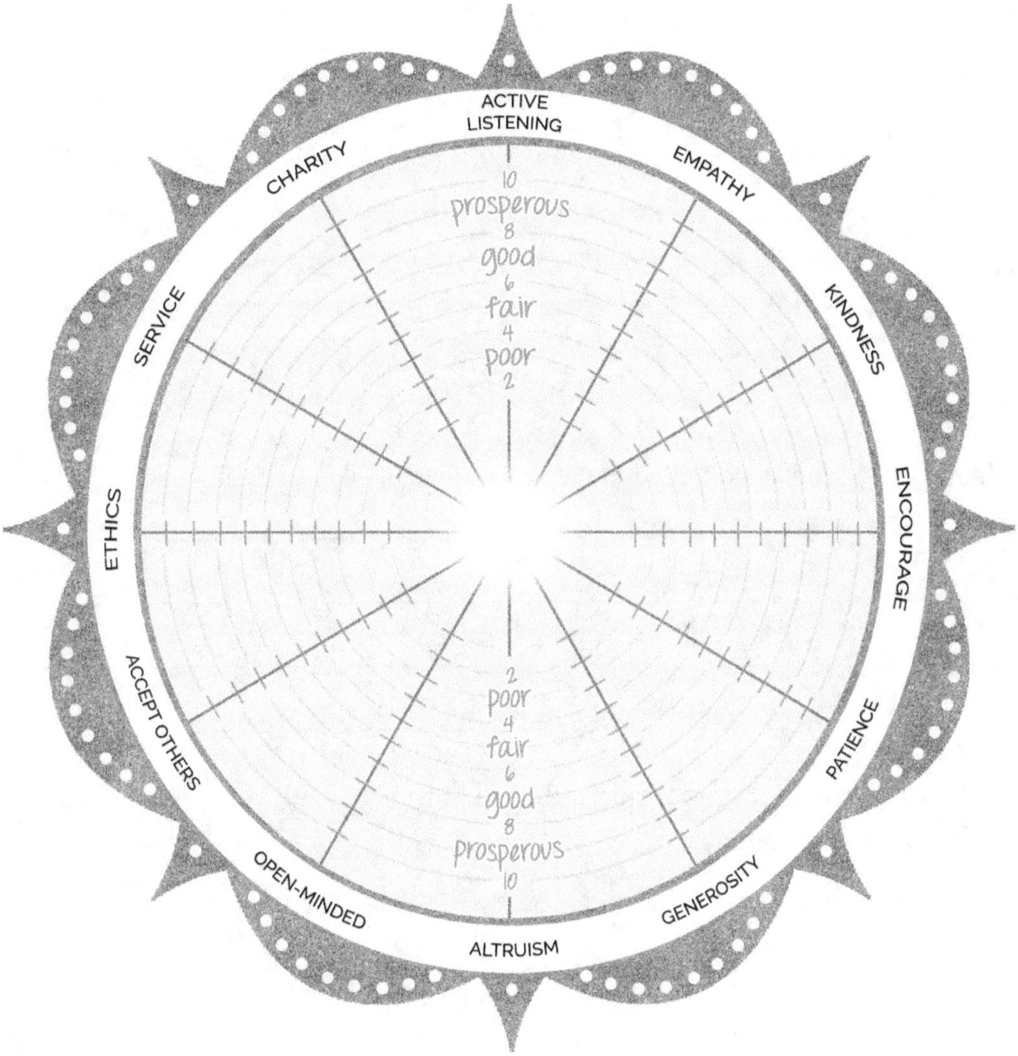

The wheel diagram labels (clockwise from top): ACTIVE LISTENING, EMPATHY, KINDNESS, ENCOURAGE, PATIENCE, GENEROSITY, ALTRUISM, OPEN-MINDED, ACCEPT OTHERS, ETHICS, SERVICE, CHARITY

Scale (top, reading inward): 10 prosperous, 8 good, 6 fair, 4 poor, 2

Scale (bottom, reading outward): 2 poor, 4 fair, 6 good, 8 prosperous, 10

The Compassion Wheel

Don't worry about your scores. We are all works in progress and have room for improvement. Just be honest. Now, answer the following questions:

> As you look at the biggest dents in your wheel, ask yourself why you scored lowest in these areas?

_____

_____

Joyce Marter, LCPC, CSP®

_____

_____

➤ Do you value these traits or not? If not, how could this be limiting your prosperity?

_____

_____

_____

_____

➤ What three action steps can you take to improve in each of these areas?

_____

_____

_____

_____

Revisit this exercise monthly or quarterly to continue to cultivate compassion. Date your wheel and file it for later reference!

Detachment

EXERCISE #1: THERAPY SESSION NUMBER 10

(Time to complete: 20 minutes)

I am excited to help you learn the art of detachment, an incredibly useful tool in work and in life. You can't detach if you are attached to expectations, outcomes, other people, money, or material possessions. Answer the following questions:

➤ Which attachment— expectations, outcomes, other people, money, or material possessions—do you most relate to?

_____

_____

_____

_____

➤ How does this attachment affect you emotionally and/or financially?

_____

_____

_____

_____

➢ If you're attached to an expectation or outcome, why can't you let it go?

_____

_____

_____

_____

➢ How might detaching improve your well-being? How might it enhance your career or financial success?

_____

_____

_____

_____

You'll be amazed to see how living with healthy detachment changes your life.

EXERCISE #2: SHELVE YOUR WORRIES WITH "THE CONTAINER"

(Time to complete: 15 minutes; lifetime practice)

EMDR therapy (Eye Movement Desensitization and Reprocessing) and other trauma protocols use The Container technique to temporarily shelve distressing thoughts or feelings in order to decrease overwhelm and increase stability and coping. This is not denial, it is healthy compartmentalization. Are you ready to give it a try? Follow these five steps:

1. Connect with your breath and do a body scan. Notice where you are holding tension, fear, or negative feelings.

2. Imagine you now have a container that is big enough and strong enough to hold these negative feelings securely.

3. Imagine putting all of your negative feelings into this container; every last bit. When you are done, close the container tightly and lock it.

4. Imagine storing your container in a safe place. Visualize sinking it to the bottom of the sea, blasting it into outer space, or handing it over to a Higher Power.

5. Remember, you can open this container again when you are ready to deal with these feelings. This could be at your next therapy session or when you are with a close friend with whom you feel comfortable talking.

EXERCISE #3: RECALIBRATE EXPECTATIONS TO ZERO

(Time to complete: 5 minutes; lifetime practice)

Before entering a meeting, going on a date, attending a family gathering, or investing in the stock market, check in with yourself about your expectations. While we want to be open to wonderful possibilities with abundant thinking, we can't attach our happiness to expectations or outcomes. So, consciously recalibrate your expectations to zero and practice gratitude for any and all good that comes.

In other words, before heading out to an event or entering an interpersonal interaction of any kind, mentally scan for any expectations you may have, mindfully let them go, and cultivate an attitude of openness and receptivity. You might be surprised by the results. Many of my clients report significant improvements in their relationships when they recalibrate expectations to zero. Give it a try!

EXERCISE #4: SEPARATE FROM NEGATIVITY

(Time to complete: 5 minutes; lifetime practice)

This is a visualization exercise. Close your eyes and spend a few minutes connecting to your breath and doing a body scan to notice where you are holding any tension or yuck. Breathe it out until you feel clear. Imagine being enveloped by a positive white light, enclosed in a safe bubble, or behind a protective, invisible shield that separates you from other people's negative feelings. When you are with others, remember this protective shield and envision their hurtful words or negative energy bouncing off the shield while you remain safe and well. This allows you to respond from a place of detachment.

EXERCISE #5: PRACTICE DETACHMENT WITH LOVE

(Time to complete: 15 minutes; lifetime practice)

Answer the following questions:

➤ Name a person in your life who you try to control. How is that working? How is that impacting your relationship? Your mental health?

_____

_____

_____

_____

➤ How would it feel to stop trying to control their behavior and focus on yourself? Is there something you would miss about the drama? If so, you need to take a deeper look and fill that void with activities and practices that are healthy for you.

_____

_____

_____

_____

➤ Name three specific controlling behaviors you are willing to let go of. Name three self-care practices you plan to increase. Try this for one week and see how detaching with love can facilitate peace and well-being with yourself and others.

_____

_____

_____

_____

EXERCISE #6: THE DETACHMENT WHEEL

(Time to complete: 20 minutes)

Date: _____

Rate your response after each question using a number from the following scale:

Poor (1-3), Fair (4-5), Good (6-7), Prosperous (8-10)									
Poor			**Fair**		**Good**			**Prosperous**	
1	2	3	4	5	6	7	8	9	10

Internal Negativity: How well are you doing at unplugging from fear, anger, sadness, doubt, worry, and financial anxiety and observing them from a neutral place? _____

External Negativity: How good are you at observing other people's emotions and maintaining a healthy separation so you can stay calm and help as needed/desired? _____

Expectation & Outcome: How good are you at detaching from outcomes and being able to trust that the result will be fine regardless of how things play out? _____

Conflict: How good are you at unlocking horns and using detachment to react from a thoughtful, compassionate place? _____

Money: How successful are you at not attaching your sense of well-being to money or material possessions? _____

Embrace Uncertainty: How successful are you at welcoming endless possibilities and the curiosity of the unknown to foster spontaneity, creativity, growth, and discovery? _____

Accept Impermanence: How well do you embrace change in this constantly changing world? _____

Not Control Others: How good are you doing when it comes to realizing you don't have power over other people's health or happiness and not trying to control them? _____

Zooming Out: How good are you at taking a step back to see situations from a greater perspective instead of through your emotions? _____

Equanimity: How well are you doing when it comes to maintaining mental calmness and an even temper during challenging situations? _____

Joyce Marter, LCPC, CSP®

Emotional Intelligence: How compassionate and effective are you when it comes to managing your emotional process and disengaging from the emotional process of others? _____

Risk Tolerance: This spoke is related to The Financial Health Wheel you completed in the introduction. Are you able to accept uncertainty when making financial decisions that involve the possibility of loss? Having the proper amount of insurance may help ease some of your worries. _____

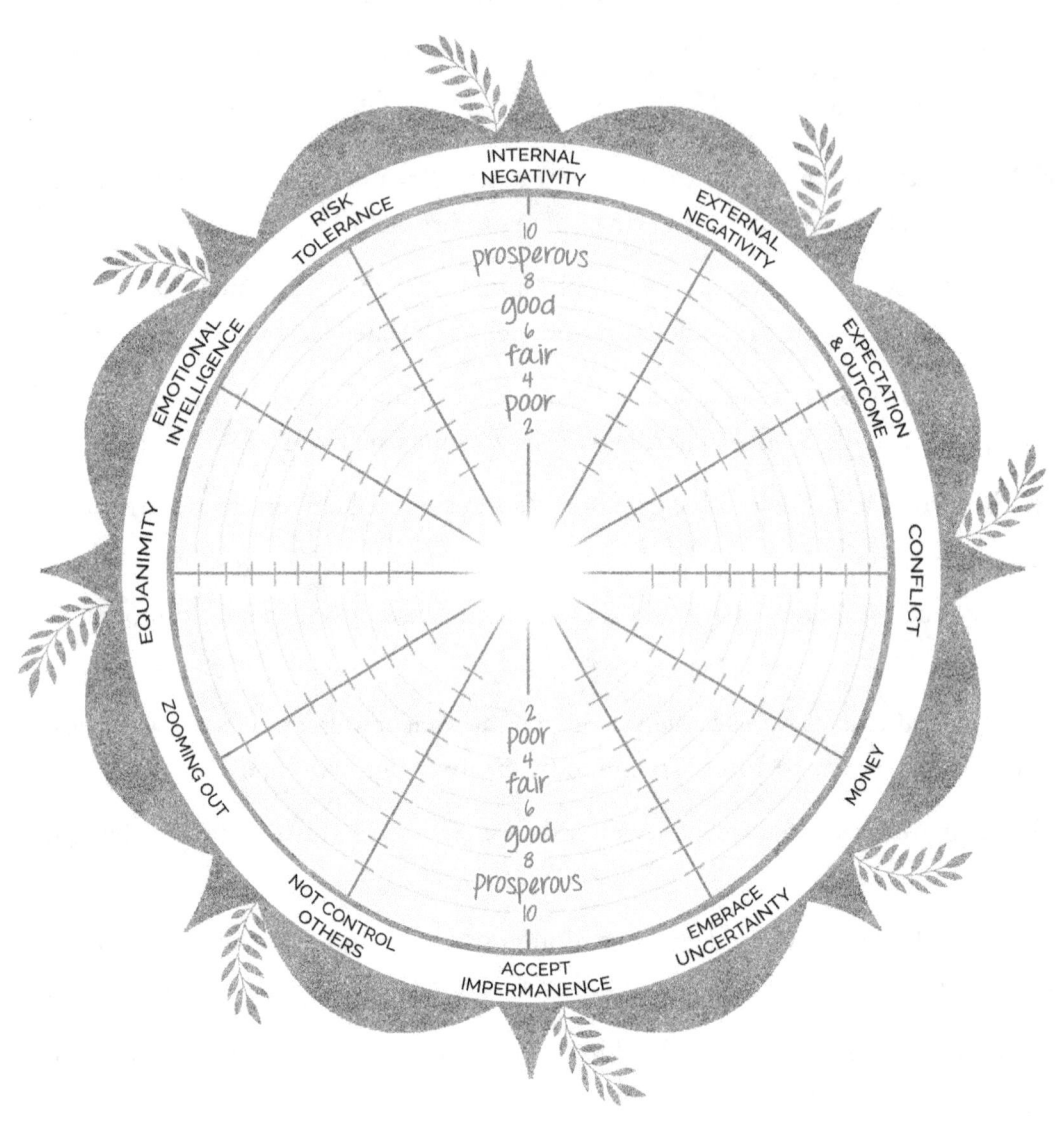

The Detachment Wheel

Chart your responses on The Detachment Wheel. Let's start at the top: are you Poor, Prosperous, or somewhere in between when it comes to Internal Negativity? Put a dot on the spoke next to the number that corresponds with your answer. Now, continue going around the wheel and after scoring yourself on every spoke, connect the dots to create a circle.

Don't worry about your scores. Just be honest. Review The Detachment Wheel and answer the following questions:

➤ Look at the three spokes with the lowest scores and list two ways you can improve in each of those areas.

_____

_____

_____

_____

➤ What are two aspects of your life where you could most benefit from healthy detachment? For example, in your partnership, parenting, or your relationship with money?

_____

_____

_____

_____

➤ In what ways would your emotional suffering decrease if you increased detachment?

_____

_____

_____

_____

Consider revisiting this exercise monthly or quarterly to continue to practice the art of detachment. Date your wheel and file it for later reference! Nice work.

Joyce Marter, LCPC, CSP®

Positivity

EXERCISE #1: THERAPY SESSION NUMBER 11

(Time to complete: 20 minutes)

In today's session, we are turning up the volume on your positivity! Answer the following questions:

➤ If you have a negative narrative in your head, how can you Weaken the Fiction?

_____

_____

_____

_____

➤ In what ways is negativity preventing your success?

_____

_____

_____

_____

➢ How might positivity open the doors to success in your life?

_____

_____

_____

_____

I am excited for you!

EXERCISE #2: REFRAME POSITIVELY TO BECOME GRATEFUL

(Time to complete: 15 minutes, lifetime practice)

Positive reframing is a technique where you try to reconsider things in a positive light to help you practice gratitude. By doing so, it can powerfully transform your thinking.

Let's positively reframe some upcoming challenges for you. Here are a couple examples to get you started:

An upcoming challenge could be a dreaded meeting with your counselor at the consumer credit agency to talk about your credit card balances, which have gotten much higher since your last meeting. A positive reframe could be being grateful for having dedicated time with a professional to help you improve your financial state.

- Another upcoming challenge could be a meeting with your boss about your low sales last month. A positive reframe could be being grateful for having a mentor and the opportunity to share and get feedback on your new sales strategy moving forward.

Now it's your turn.

➤ List three upcoming challenges or obstacles. Make sure at least one pertains to your career or finances.

_____

_____

_____

_____

➤ What are the reasons why this is such a challenge?

_____

_____

_____

_____

➤ Now, reframe the challenge in a positive way showing what blessings could result because of the situation.

_____

_____

_____

_____

EXERCISE #3: ACT "AS IF"

(Time to complete: 10 minutes; lifetime practice)

Give acting "as if" a try in whichever of the following ways works best for you:

➤ Record yourself (audio or video, but video is better because you can see your face when you replay it) telling a loved one of "recent accomplishments" that impacted your finances. The longer and more detailed, the better. Be sure to listen to it at least once or twice to retrain your neural pathways to think positively.

_____

_____

_____

_____

➤ Pick one trusted confidant (perhaps your partner, best friend, or therapist) and act "as if" you accomplished your goals for one to five minutes. Ask them for feedback, for example, if you seemed happy and excited.

_____

_____

_____

_____

Then, write about what this assignment was like for you. How did it feel to speak as if you had achieved your dreams? Was it uncomfortable at first and then did it become easier?

EXERCISE #4: LOOK FOR THE EXCEPTIONS

(Time to complete: 10 minutes; lifetime practice)

Answer the following questions:

➢ What's a current problem you are facing?

_____

_____

_____

_____

➢ Can you remember a time when this problem wasn't happening?

_____

_____

_____

_____

➢ What was different then?

_____

_____

_____

_____

➢ What were you *doing* differently?

_____

_____

_____

_____

➤ How were you *thinking* differently?

_____

_____

_____

_____

➤ What can you do differently *now* because of this exception?

_____

_____

_____

_____

EXERCISE #5: DO SOME EXPOSURE THERAPY

(Time to complete: 20 minutes; lifetime practice)

This exercise is based on systematic desensitization, a behavioral therapy technique used for treating phobias and anxiety. The idea is to expand your comfort zone by getting used to things that make you uncomfortable. Do the following:

➤ Name three activities outside your comfort zone that are important for your career success in the near future.

_____

_____

_____

_____

➤ Pick one of these activities that is particularly relevant and important. What resources and skills do you need to successfully accomplish this activity?

_____

_____

_____

_____

➤ Make a plan and set an intention for pursuing this activity in the near future. For example, if you have a fear of public speaking, join a Toastmasters group or take an improv comedy class.

_____

_____

_____

_____

➢ Set a target date for completing the activity and ask a trusted confidant to hold you accountable and support you in this endeavor.

_____

_____

_____

_____

EXERCISE #6: THE WORK SATISFACTION WHEEL

(Time to complete: 20 minutes)

Date: _____

Rate your response after each question using a number from the following scale:

Poor (1-3), Fair (4-5), Good (6-7), Prosperous (8-10)									
Poor			**Fair**			**Good**		**Prosperous**	
1	2	3	4	5	6	7	8	9	10

Salary/Pay: Jot down the amount of compensation you receive including your salary or pay, plus any commissions or bonuses on the lines outside this spoke. How prosperous is your current compensation? _____

Health Benefits: List your current health-care benefits including medical, vision, and dental plans, a health savings account, or other perks like gym access. How prosperous are you in health-care benefits? _____

Retirement Benefits: Write down your current retirement benefits including your ability to invest (not how much you have invested) in pre-tax earnings into a 401(k) plan (in for-profit settings), 403(b) plan (in nonprofit or government settings), or Roth IRA (self-employed settings). How prosperous are you in accessing retirement benefits? _____

Time Off: Jot down how much flexibility you have to take time off, whether or not it is paid time off and how much time you can take off for vacations, sick days, and other leaves of absence. How prosperous are you when it comes to taking time off? _____

Ownership/Interest: Write down notes about your ability to become a partner or owner, obtain stock options, or have a vested interest in your place of work. How prosperous are you in your ability to have ownership or a vested interest? _____

Enjoyment: Jot down the aspects of your job you enjoy or don't enjoy. How prosperous are you in terms of deriving pleasure and enjoyment from your work? _____

Meaning: List which aspects of your work are meaningful and rewarding to you on a deeper level. How prosperous are you when it comes to finding meaning in your work? _____

Self-Alignment: Mark down your unique gifts and talents, core values, and mission in the world. How prosperous are you in your work aligning with your true self? _____

Work-Life Balance: Write down the aspects of flexibility or lack thereof in your current work situation. This includes the ability to work from home, flexible hours, work-life balance, commute time, or required travel. _____

Appreciation: List the ways you are acknowledged for your efforts and achievements, including words of affirmation, appropriate title, awards, or special perks. How prosperous are you in appreciation and recognition at work? _____

Professional Growth: Jot down your current opportunities for professional growth including mentoring, continuing education, or other alternative opportunities for learning. How prosperous are you in opportunities for professional development? _____

Connect to Colleagues: Write notes about how your work does or does not foster collaboration, social support, and a sense of belonging. How prosperous are you in connection to colleagues?

_____

Chart your numbered responses and then connect the dots. Start at the top: are you Poor, Prosperous, or somewhere in between when it comes to negotiating Salary/Pay? Put a dot on the spoke next to the number that corresponds with your answer. Now, continue going around the wheel and after scoring yourself on every spoke, connect the dots to create a circle.

The Work Satisfaction Wheel

At the end of each spoke, list what's important to you under each of the categories. To get you started with ideas, see The Work Satisfaction Wheel Example.

The wheel diagram contains the following handwritten annotations positioned around it:

- $50K per year / $2K bonus / Wish I made $25K
- Love my work fam
- Health insurance / Vision and dental / Flex spending / Would prefer PPO option
- Trainings / Wish they would pay for / my masters
- 401K with matching
- None other than paycheck / Would like a title change
- 15 days PTO per year
- 80 hour work week / On call / Not much PTO - want 4 weeks / Want 40-50 hour workweek
- (none)
- Fits with my values / but doesn't use my / leadership skills
- Enjoy facilitating groups
- Very rewarding work

Wheel spoke labels (clockwise): SALARY/PAY, HEALTH BENEFITS, RETIREMENT BENEFITS, TIME OFF, OWNERSHIP / INTEREST, ENJOYMENT, MEANING, SELF-ALIGNMENT, WORK-LIFE BALANCE, APPRECIATION, PROFESSIONAL GROWTH, CONNECT TO COLLEAGUES

Scale (top): 10 prosperous / 8 good / fair 4 / poor 2
Scale (bottom): 2 poor / 4 fair / good 8 / prosperous 10

The Work Satisfaction Wheel Example

In The Work Satisfaction Wheel Example, notice the two deepest dents in the wheel are in the areas of Work-Life Balance and Ownership/Vested Interest. These would be the areas of needed improvement or negotiation.

After filling your wheel in completely, answer the following questions:

➤ To see your overall satisfaction with your work, add up your total spoke scores and divide the total by twelve. Is it closer to the Poor or the Prosperous range?

_____

_____

➤ What are your three lowest ratings or dents on the wheel?

_____

_____

_____

_____

➤ Can you negotiate for more of this at your current workplace? Or create it for yourself somehow?

_____

_____

_____

_____

➤ Can you attain greater prosperity in your current work or do you need to make some changes? Write out your thoughts and an action plan. Include details about what your ideal situation would look like.

_____

_____

_____

_____

Consider revisiting this exercise at least twice a year so you can continue to advocate for yourself. The more you work at it, the better you'll become at it. Date your wheel and file it for later reference!

EXERCISE #7: THE POSITIVITY WHEEL

(Time to complete: 20 minutes)

Date: _____

Rate your response after each question using a number from the following scale:

Poor (1-3), Fair (4-5), Good (6-7), Prosperous (8-10)									
Poor			**Fair**			**Good**		**Prosperous**	
1	2	3	4	5	6	7	8	9	10

Positive Psychology: Focusing on the strengths and gifts that enable you and others to thrive and succeed. When it comes to answering the proverbial question, "Is your glass half empty or half full?" how would you rate yourself at being half full? _____

Weaken the Fiction: Identifying and overcoming excuses or negative narratives you tell yourself that are between you and the success you deserve. How successful are you at WTF? _____

Gratitude: Expressing thanks and appreciation. How successful are you at taking the time to reflect on what you are grateful for? _____

Positive Reframing: How would you rate yourself when it comes to looking at the good parts of any situation? _____

Cheerful: Expressing happiness, joy, humor, and good spirits. When it comes to expressing cheerful vibes, how would you rate yourself? _____

Optimism: Being hopeful and confident about the future; expecting a favorable outcome. How optimistic are you about the future? _____

Passion: Bringing excited energy to what you do. How passionate are you about being positive? _____

Courage: Doing something that frightens you; expanding your comfort zone. When it comes to being courageous, how would you rate yourself? _____

Action: Identifying opportunities and taking steps to achieve them. How would you rate yourself when it comes to taking action? _____

Creativity: Utilizing positive energy to develop original thoughts, ideas, or innovations. How would you rate yourself when it comes to creativity? _____

Solution-Focused: Focusing on building strengths and finding solutions rather than just discussing problems. How would you rate yourself at being solution focused? _____

Negotiate: How good are you at advocating for yourself in your work and financial life to arrive at win-win agreements? _____

The Positivity Wheel

Chart your responses on The Positivity Wheel. Start at the top: are you Poor, Prosperous, or somewhere in between when it comes to embracing Positive Psychology? Put a dot on the spoke next to the number that corresponds with your answer. Now, continue going around the wheel and after scoring yourself on every spoke, connect the dots to create a circle.

We all can use a little more positivity in our lives. Consider revisiting this exercise monthly or quarterly to continue to keep increasing your positivity. Date your wheel and file it for later reference!

Answer the following questions:

➢ As you look at the biggest dents in your wheel, notice which areas you scored yourself the lowest. Why do you think this is so?

_____

_____

_____

_____

➢ How might working on these areas improve your personal life? Professional life? Financial life?

_____

_____

_____

_____

➢ What three action steps can you take to improve in each of these three areas?

_____

_____

_____

_____

You got this! Yippee! Hurray! (Can you tell I was a high school cheerleader?)

CHAPTER -

Resilience

EXERCISE #1: THERAPY SESSION NUMBER 12

(Time to complete: 20 minutes)

This is our final session! All the skills you have learned in our work together foster resilience. Today, I'd like you to think of a significant challenge from the past that you overcame, and then answer the following questions:

➤ How did you get through it?

_____

_____

_____

_____

➤ What lessons did you learn?

_____

_____

_____

_____

➤ How might these lessons help you develop financial resilience?

_____

_____

_____

_____

➤ You're doing such important self-reflection! Wonderful work.

_____

_____

_____

_____

EXERCISE #2: FLAGGING THE MINEFIELD

(Time to complete: 10 minutes; lifetime practice)

To get started, consider a time when you faced a big challenge and were able to manage it successfully because you planned for it. You used a technique used in solution-focused brief therapy called Flagging the Minefield.

Want to give it a try? You can practice this by identifying any upcoming stressful situations and proactively thinking about which coping strategies you can use to move through them successfully.

I've done this by going as far as to flag certain times of the year that may be more stressful for me. For example, as a mom, September, December, and May seem to be the busiest times of year, so I plan to not overextend myself with work and to build in extra time for self-care. From a financial perspective, my therapy practice is the slowest during December and August, which used to cause me financial anxiety until I flagged it and planned for it, by using that time of year for my own vacations as my clients weren't coming in then anyway.

Answer the following questions:

➢ In looking at the week or month ahead, write down three upcoming events that you anticipate will be stressful. Make sure at least one is financial, such as paying your bills or reviewing your budget.

_____

_____

_____

➢ For each upcoming event that you have flagged, write down three strategies that have helped you successfully cope with these types of situations in the past. For example, you went for a run before doing your bills or rewarded yourself by meeting up with friends afterward.

_____

_____

_____

_____

➢ Now, schedule in time for your coping strategies before or after the stressful event.

_____

_____

_____

_____

➢ Congratulations on having prepared to be resilient!

_____

_____

_____

_____

EXERCISE #3: CREATE A FINANCIAL RESILIENCE PLAN

(Time to complete: 20 minutes; lifetime practice)

Answer the following questions:

➤ In what ways might financial resilience improve your situation?

_____

_____

_____

_____

➤ How well are you doing at following the budget you created in chapter 2? Are there any changes you need to make to help you live below your means so you can save more money?

_____

_____

_____

_____

➤ Do you have an emergency fund? If so, is it enough to pay three to six months' worth of expenses? If not, what is a realistic goal for bolstering your emergency fund? What are two concrete steps you can take to achieve this goal?

_____

_____

_____

_____

➢ In the event of an adverse financial event, who would you turn to for emotional, financial, or logistical support? What can you do now to strengthen your social capital to prepare for hard times?

_____

_____

_____

_____

EXERCISE #4: FOCUS ON GROWTH

(Time to complete: 15 minutes; lifetime practice)

Answer the following questions:

➢ What are your expectations for making progress in your career, business, or finances? Do you expect your progress to be linear or do you envision many ups and downs on the road to success?

_____

_____

_____

_____

➢ Have you ever experienced Apex of the Mountain Syndrome (i.e., self-doubt prior to a major accomplishment)?

_____

_____

_____

_____

➢ Do you tend to frame major setbacks as a learning experience? What might be the value of developing a growth mindset in response to setbacks you may face in the future?

_____

_____

_____

_____

EXERCISE #5: PRACTICE AFFIRMATIONS FOR RESILIENCE

(Time to complete: 10 minutes; lifetime practice)

Practice some affirmations to continue to foster resilience:

- I made it through challenges in the past and I trust that I will again.

- I am bendable and flexible like a reed in the wind. (This is my husband's favorite affirmation, which he created!)

- I am open and adaptable.

- I am growing, evolving, and thriving.

- I will persevere and prosper.

- I claim my personal power and refuse to give it away to others.

- I share my talents and gifts openly and brightly. I refuse to make myself small or less-than for the sake of not threatening others.

- I shine the unique light of my spirit with brilliance and magnificence.

- I use my voice to speak honestly and directly for my mind, my heart, and my gut.

- Because I love myself, I regularly ask for what I want, need, hope, desire, and dream.

- I trust that I will survive and manage all that comes and refuse to succumb to the fear of rejection or failure.

- I express love openly and freely with awesome vulnerability and joy.

- I set healthy boundaries personally and professionally and say no as needed.

- I actively seek work, hobbies, and relationships that are meaningful to me and nurturing to my soul, and free myself from commitments that bind my spirit.

- I welcome new experiences, relationships, and opportunities that will expand my comfort zone.

- I practice self-compassion and self-acceptance and lovingly melt away any shame, embarrassment, or insecurity to prevent me from being my highest and best self.

- I free myself from the powers of fear and doubt. I choose love, faith, and courage as my guides.

EXERCISE #6: THE RESILIENCE WHEEL

(Time to complete: 20 minutes)

Date: _____

Rate your response after each question using a number from the following scale:

Poor (1-3), Fair (4-5), Good (6-7), Prosperous (8-10)									
Poor			**Fair**			**Good**		**Prosperous**	
1	2	3	4	5	6	7	8	9	10

Challenges as Opportunities: How well are you able to look at the upsides and blessings that come with adversity? _____

Trust the Process: How well are you doing with maintaining faith in a positive outcome while navigating challenges and inevitable delays throughout the process? _____

Adaptable: How well are you able to internally adjust to any new conditions in your life or work so you can continue to thrive? _____

Flexible: How open-minded and willing to compromise with others are you while on the road to success? Are you willing to make necessary changes to your initial plan without giving up?

_____

Strength: How strong do you feel in mind, body, and spirit? How much grit do you possess?

_____

Motivation: How driven and determined are you in your mission to achieve your goals?

_____

Growth Mindset: How well do you frame setbacks and failures as normal aspects of growth?

_____

Financial Resilience: How well have you done at creating an emergency fund and diversifying investments, personal, and social capital so you can move through financial challenges and continue to thrive? _____

Avoid Comparing: How well do you avoid comparing yourself to others as you pursue your goals? _____

Bounce Back: How easily do you typically return to your usual functioning after a challenging event or experience? How well do you get back up after setbacks such as a job loss, a breakup, an illness, or other life challenge? _____

Persevere: Perseverance is the determination to stick to something and stay on course in spite of obstacles. How likely are you to continue to strive to achieve your goals despite difficulties or delays? _____

Transform: How good are you at using your resilience to create personal, professional, and financial growth and evolution in your life? _____

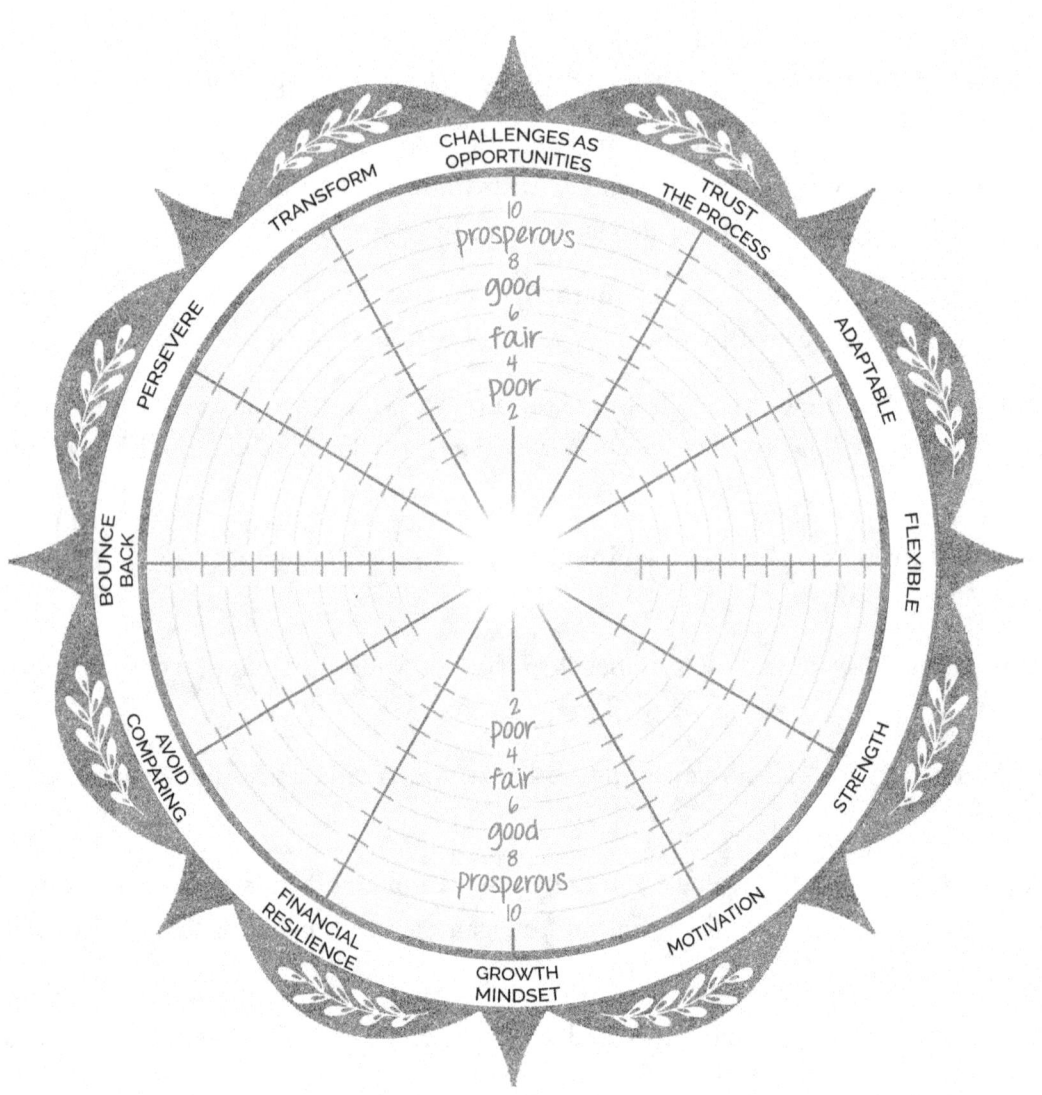

The Resilience Wheel

Chart your responses on The Resilience Wheel. Let's start at the top: are you Poor, Prosperous, or somewhere in between when it comes to viewing Challenges as Opportunities? Put a dot on the spoke next to the number that corresponds with your answer. Now, continue going around the wheel and after scoring yourself on every spoke, connect the dots to create a circle.

Answer the following questions:

➢ Look at the dents in your wheel and notice which three areas you need the most improvement when it comes to resilience?

_____

_____

_____

_____

➢ How have you improved your resilience since you started this program?

_____

_____

_____

_____

➢ In what ways do you plan to continue to foster resilience in your life?

_____

_____

_____

_____

Date your wheel and file it for later reference. Consider revisiting this exercise monthly or quarterly to keep building your resilience. Soon you will be a resilience rock star!

Congratulations on completing this program! I can't wait to see your progress as we wrap everything up in the conclusion. Let's see what you've accomplished!

Joyce Marter, LCPC, CSP®

Conclusion

FINANCIAL MINDSET WISDOM: BRINGING IT ALL TOGETHER FOR COMPLETE PROSPERITY

Congratulations for making this commitment to your financial mindset. By working through this program, you've got everything you need to be successful in work and life. What have you learned? Are you talking the talk as well as walking the walk? It's time to see how far you've come.

EXERCISE #1: THE MINDSET FIX WHEEL

(Time to complete: 20 minutes)

Date: _____

Rate your response after each question using a number from the following scale:

Poor (1-3), Fair (4-5), Good (6-7), Prosperous (8-10)									
Poor			**Fair**			**Good**		**Prosperous**	
1	**2**	**3**	**4**	**5**	**6**	**7**	**8**	**9**	**10**

Consider each of the chapter's mindsets in this book as one small slice of the Mindset Fix Wheel:

Abundance: How successful have you been at shifting your thoughts of scarcity to abundance?

_____

Awareness: How successful have you been at consciously breaking habit and thought patterns and choosing a more prosperous path? How are you doing with being aware of your mental health? How are you doing at breaking through defenses and denial? _____

Responsibility: How successful have you been at freeing yourself of resentment and anger by taking responsibility and granting forgiveness? _____

Presence: How good are you at giving yourself the present of presence to experience the riches only available in the here and now? _____

Essence: How connected do you feel with your inner light and highest self? _____

270 The Financial Mindset Fix

Self-Love: How good are you at practicing self-care, self-affirmation, and self-compassion? How well are you silencing your Inner Saboteur? _____

Vision: How successful have you been at recreating your life in new and magical ways by envisioning the streets paved with gold? _____

Support: How successful have you been at opening yourself up to receiving support, weeding out toxic relationships, and welcoming supportive people into your life to do more good in the world? _____

Compassion: How good have you been at opening your mind, encouraging others, and paying it forward with generosity? ____

Detachment: How good are you at detaching from drama and negativity and staying on course?

____

Positivity: How good have you been at spinning straw into gold by practicing gratitude in order to attract greater prosperity? ____

Resilience: How are you doing when it comes to resilience? Are you better able to bounce back from challenges and thrive? Are you transforming into your best self in the process?

____

Chart your responses on the Mindset Fix Wheel. Start at the top: are you Poor, Prosperous, or somewhere in between when it comes to Abundance? Put a dot on the spoke next to the number that corresponds with your answer. Now, continue going around the wheel and after scoring yourself on every spoke, connect the dots to create a circle.

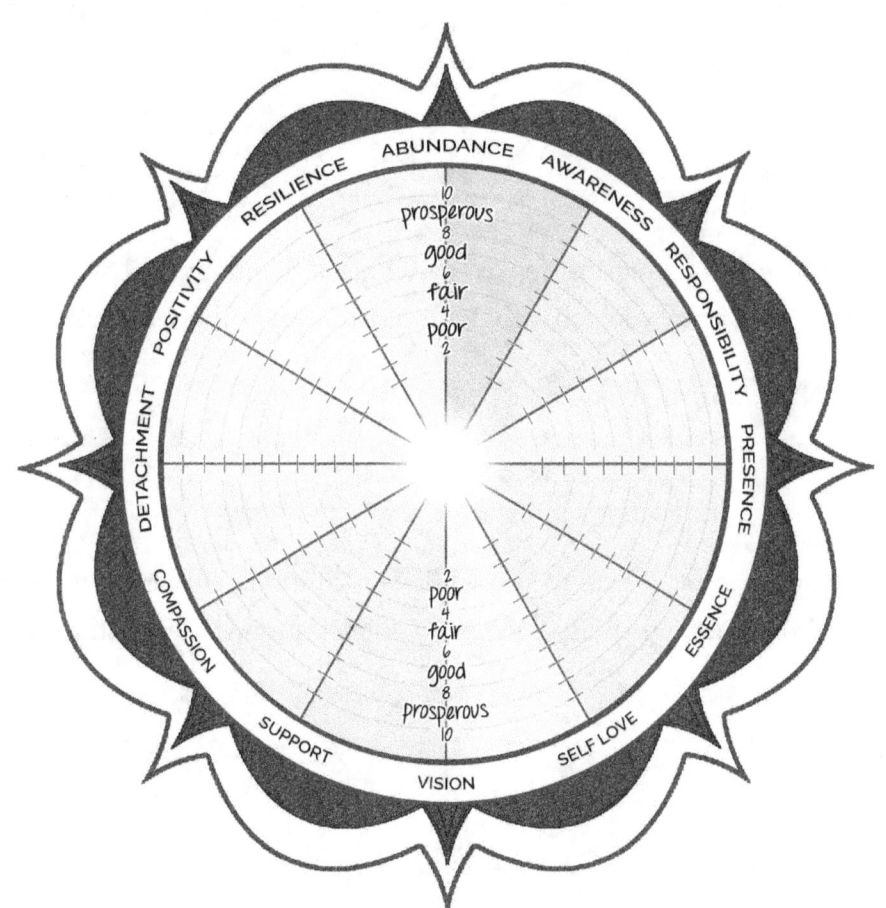

The Mindset Fix Wheel

Look at your wheel and think about how much you have improved in each area since starting this program. To keep yourself on track, consider completing this exercise once a quarter so you can live more consciously.

Your journey doesn't end here. A financial mindset is not a finite accomplishment, it is a way of living. As life throws you challenges, there will be dents in your wheel—that's okay and natural. You've got all the tools you need to keep working as you continue to strive for balance, wholeness, and greater prosperity. We are all works in progress striving toward greater mental and financial health.

Answer the following questions:

➤ Which three mindsets are the strongest for you and why? How can those strengths help bolster less strong areas?

_____

_____

_____

_____

➤ What are your lowest-scoring spokes (the biggest dents in your wheel)? Why do you think this is? What are you going to do to continue to build these mindsets?

_____

_____

_____

➤ What would be most helpful to you while you continue to work through the program? Do you need an accountability partner or a small group to work through the program together?

_____

_____

_____

EXERCISE #2: THE FINANCIAL HEALTH WHEEL

(Time to complete: 20 minutes)

At the beginning of this program, you completed your Financial Health Wheel, pulling it out for reference. Each spoke of The Financial Health Wheel applies to a spoke in each of the chapter's wheels. To refresh your memory, I've included the chapter in which you worked on this skill. Let's look at how your financial health has improved since you started working through the program.

Date: _____

Rate your response after each question using a number from the following scale:

Poor (1-3), Fair (4-5), Good (6-7), Prosperous (8-10)			
Poor	**Fair**	**Good**	**Prosperous**
1　　2　　3	4　　5	6　　7　　8	9　　10

Own Your Worth: How deserving do you feel of achieving greater financial prosperity? (Abundance) _____

Budget: How aware are you of your spending versus your budget? How successful are you at avoiding financial denial? (Awareness) _____

Timely Bill Pay: How good are you at taking responsibility for organizing and paying your bills on time? (Responsibility) _____

Spend within Means: How mindful are you of your spending habits and spending within your limits so that you do not accrue debt? (Presence) _____

Know Your Net Worth: How aware are you of your approximate net worth at any given time? Net worth is the calculation of all your assets (bank account balances, value investments, property, etc.) minus your liabilities (credit card balances, loans, mortgages, etc.). (Essence, Not Ego) _____

Treat Yourself: How good are you treating yourself within your means? Just like a healthy diet allows for the occasional cheat day (which actually keeps you satisfied and sticking to the overall plan), it's okay to treat yourself. (Self-Love) _____

Joyce Marter, LCPC, CSP®

Financial Planning: How are you doing with planning for your financial health, including paying off student loans or credit card debt and saving to buy a home, kids' college, or retirement? (Vision) _____

Financial Advisor Check-Ins: How are you doing with making an appointment with your financial advisor once or twice a year to keep you on track? (Support) _____

Charity: How are you doing when it comes to supporting causes that are meaningful to you in a doable way? If your finances are tight, are you giving in other ways such as volunteering your time, donating unneeded items, or promoting awareness of these causes through social media or other formats? (Compassion) _____

Negotiate: How good are you at negotiating better pay or benefits, major purchases, or bartering services to get deals? (Positivity) _____

Risk Tolerance: How close are you to having the proper amount of insurance for your health, car, house or apartment, business, and even your life? (Detachment) _____

Save & Invest: How close are to having three months to six months of emergency savings and are you investing money for your future? Remember, having savings allows you to persevere through unexpected challenges, such as a job loss. (Resilience) _____

Chart your responses on The Financial Health Wheel. Start at the top: are you Poor, Prosperous, or somewhere in between when it comes to being able to Own Your Worth? Put a dot on the spoke next to the number that corresponds with your answer. Now, continue going around the wheel and after scoring yourself on every spoke, connect the dots to create a circle.

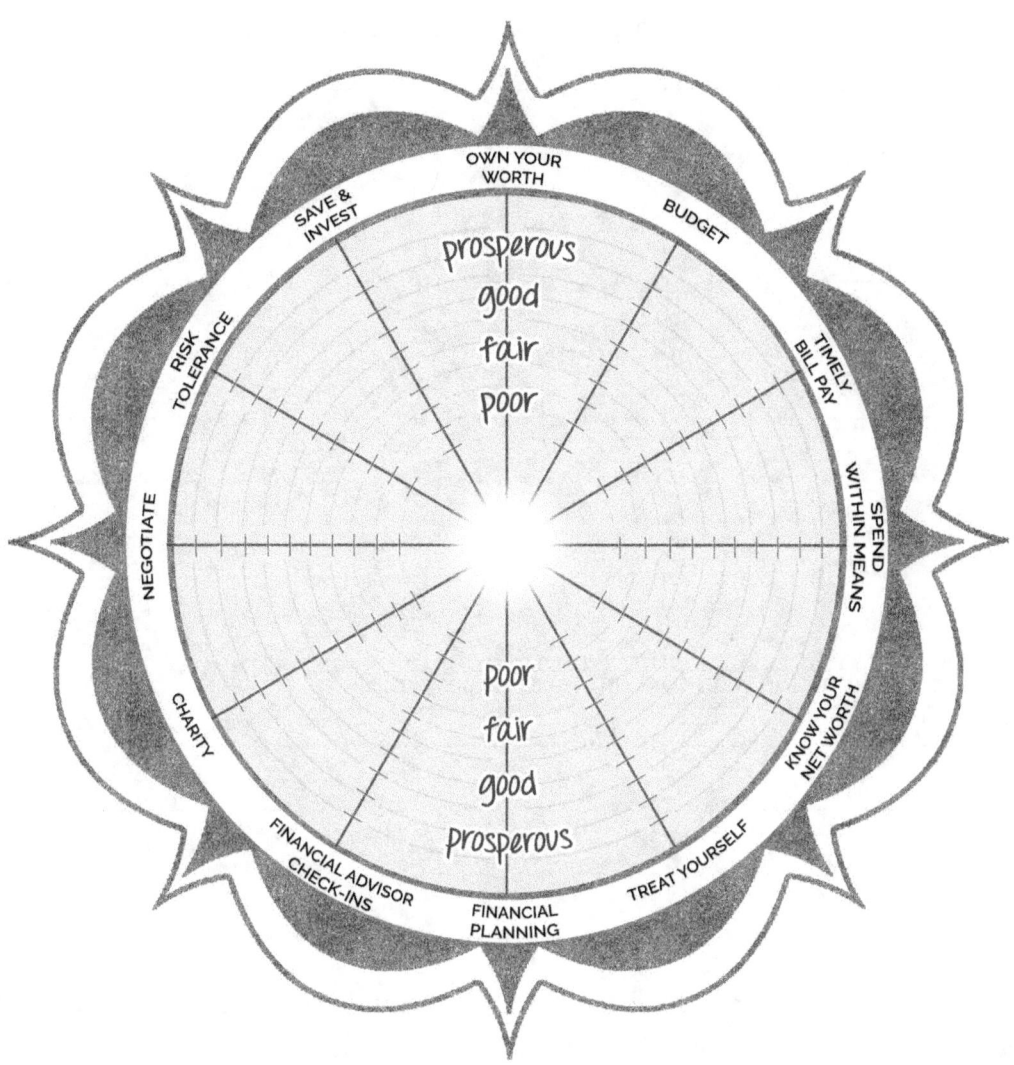

The Financial Health Wheel

Compare The Financial Health Wheel you completed at the beginning of the program to see your progress. Write your responses to the following questions:

> In which three areas did you most improve? How does that feel?

_____

_____

_____

_____

➤ What would you like to do to build on or celebrate this improvement?

_____

_____

_____

_____

➤ Which three areas need ongoing attention (the biggest dents in the wheel)?

_____

_____

_____

_____

➤ What is your action plan for continued improvement?

_____

_____

_____

_____

Date your wheel and file it for later reference as you witness how your financial mindset continues to increase your financial health. Congratulations! You have now completed your final activity in this program!

(For additional practice, please click on this https://www.joyce-marter.com/exercises/ for additional exercises.)

APPENDIX:

WHEEL WORKSHEETS

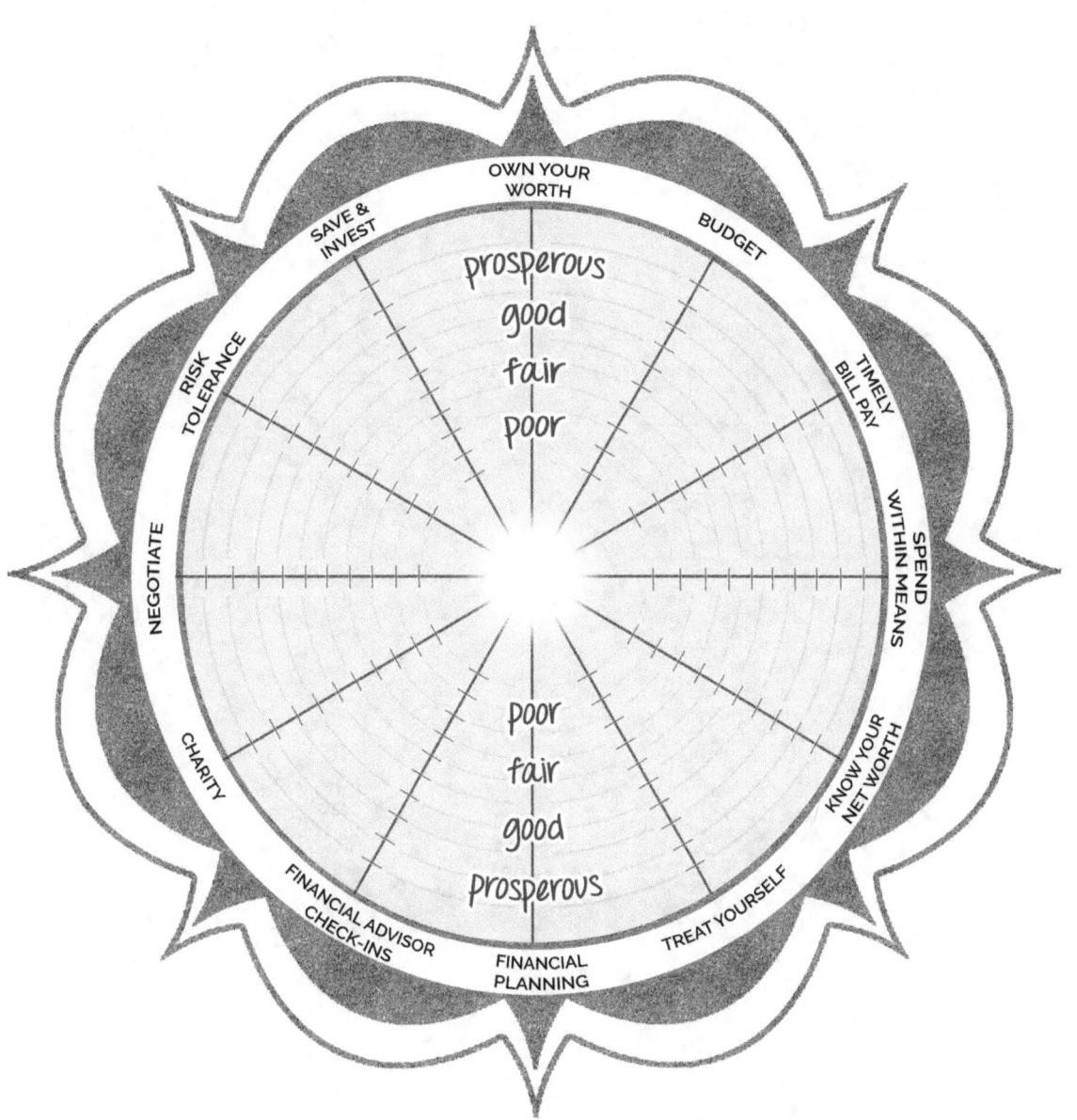

The Financial Health Wheel

Joyce Marter, LCPC, CSP®

The Abundance Wheel

The following labels appear around the wheel:

SELF-AWARENESS
RELATIONAL ROLES
FINANCIAL CONSCIOUSNESS
UNCONCIOUS CONTRACTS
MENTAL HEALTH
DEFENSIVE MECHANISMS
PHYSICAL HEALTH
SUBSTANCE USE
STRESSORS
ADDICTIONS
ATTACHMENT STYLE
TRAUMAS

Top scale (reading outward from center):
10 prosperous
8 good
6 fair
4 poor
2

Bottom scale (reading outward from center):
2 poor
4 fair
6 good
8 prosperous
10

The Awareness Wheel

Joyce Marter, LCPC, CSP®

The Responsibility Wheel

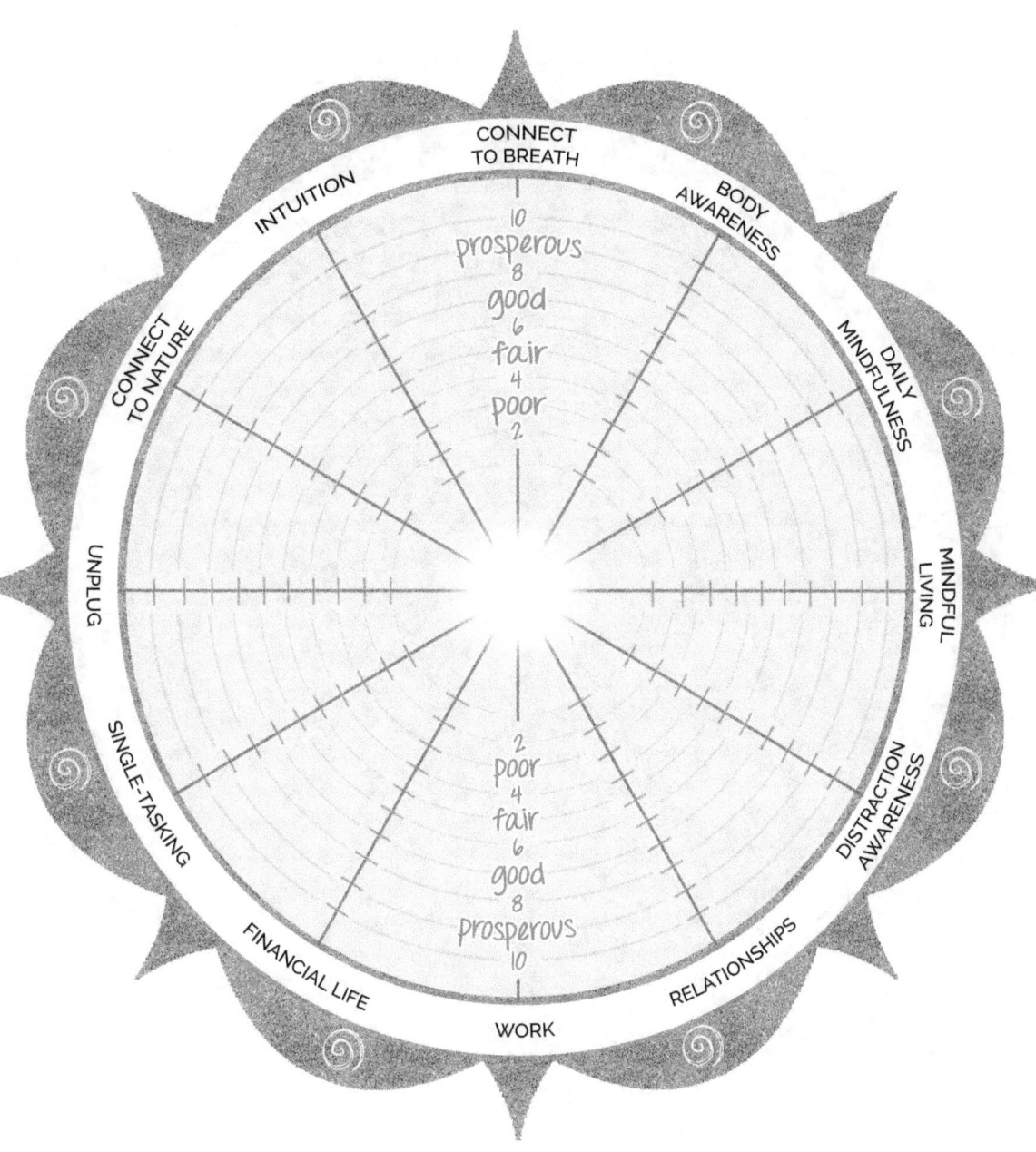

The Presence Wheel

Joyce Marter, LCPC, CSP®

The Essence Wheel

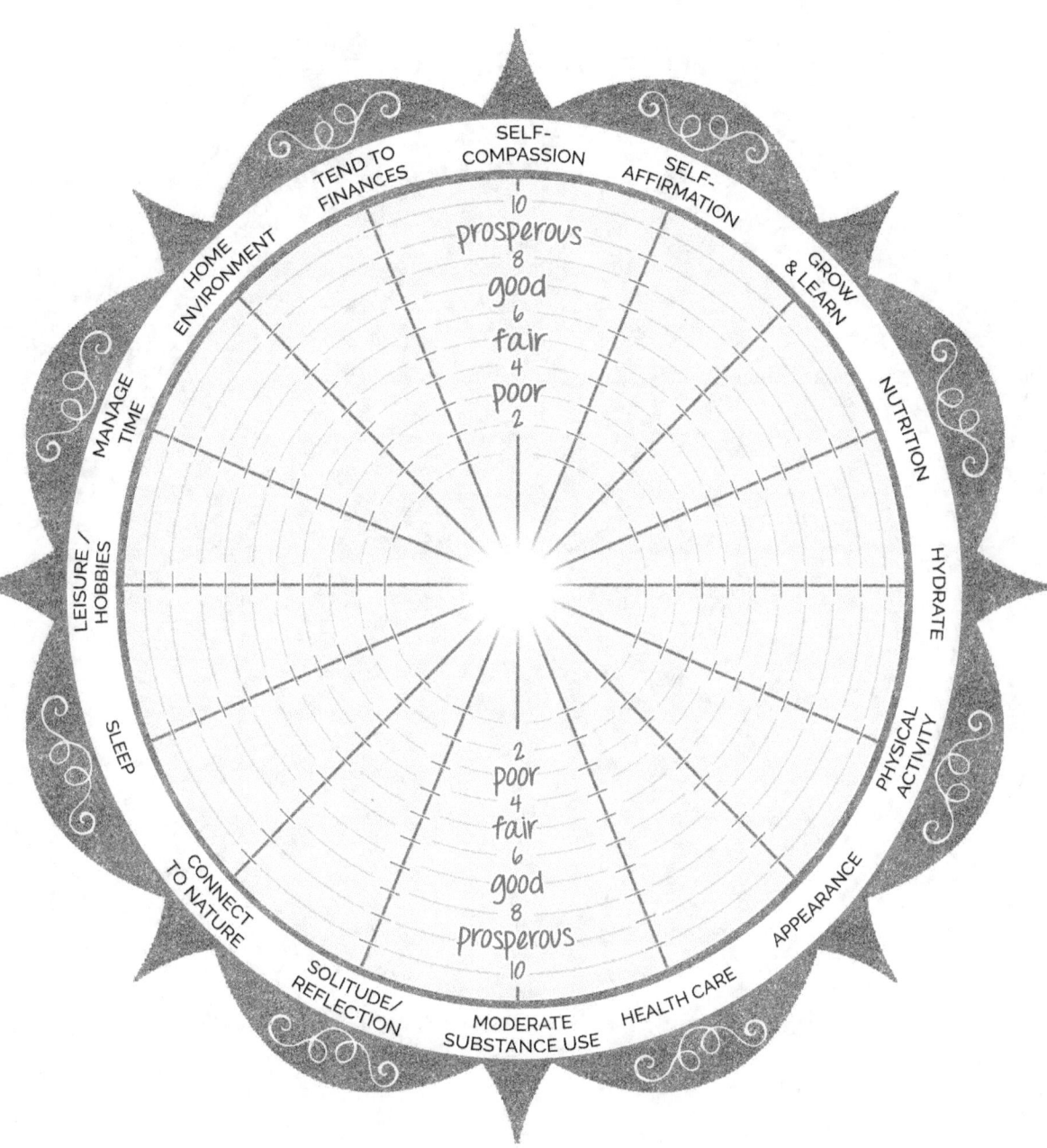

The Self-Love Wheel

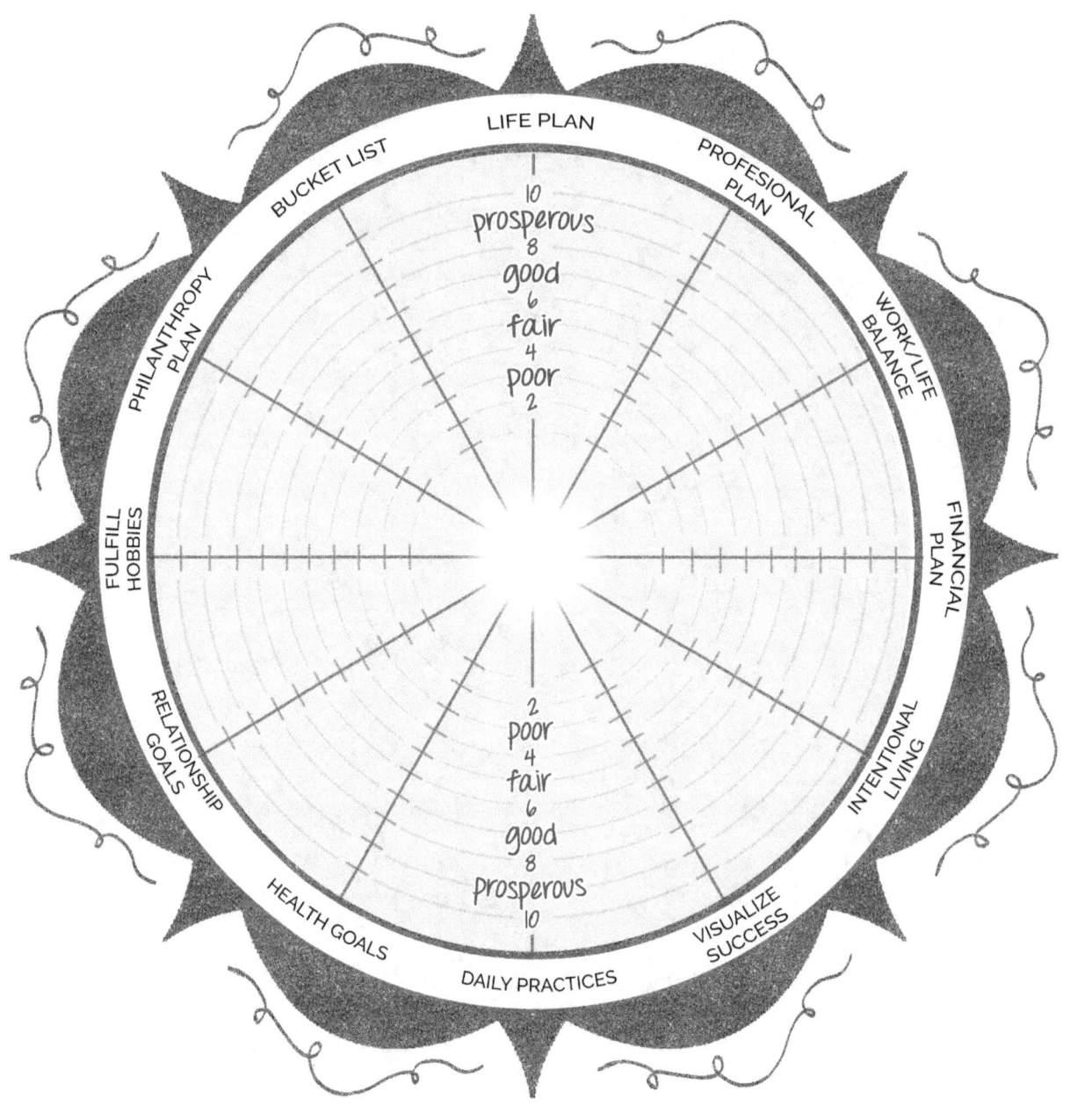

The Vision Wheel

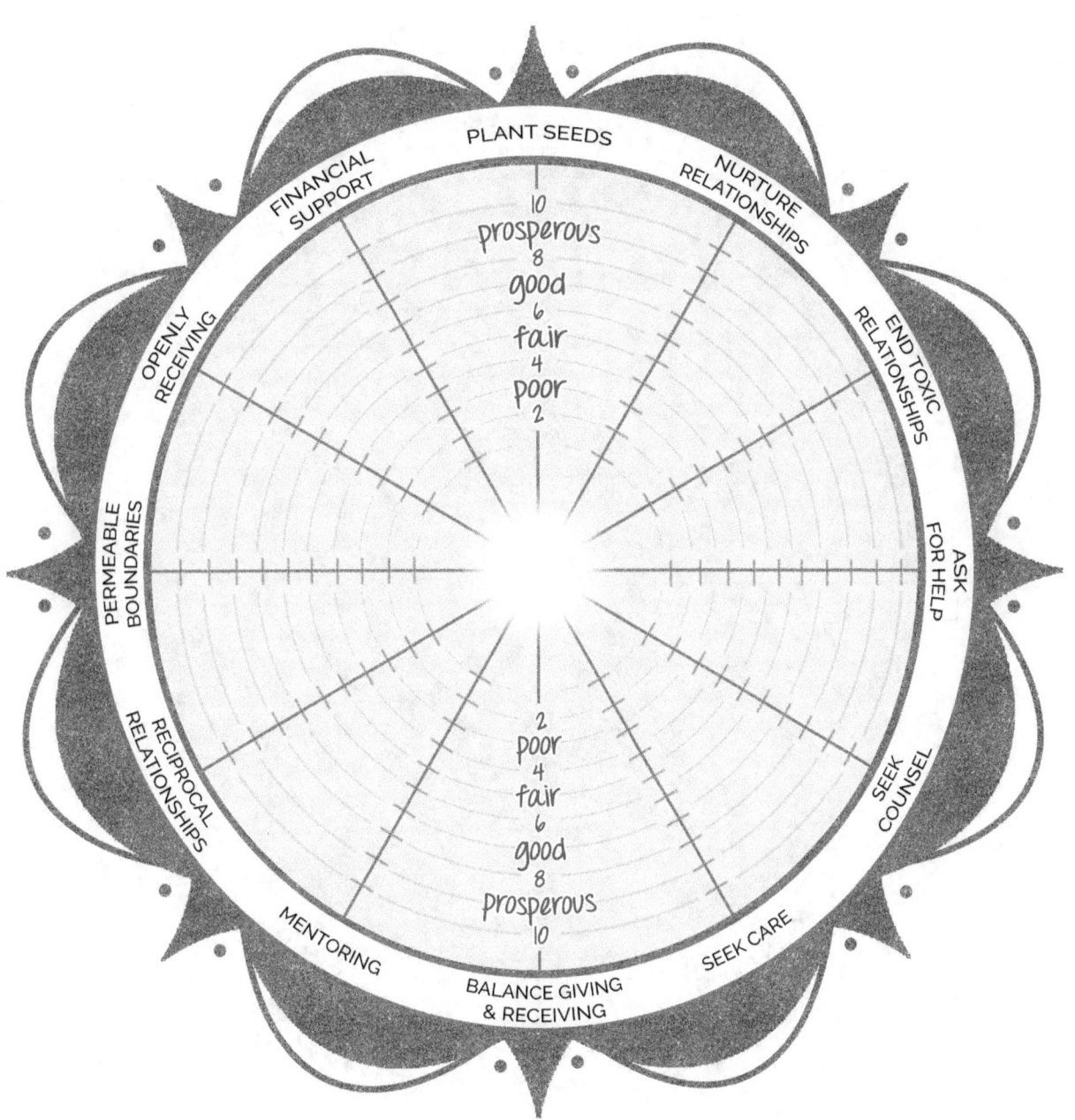

The Support Wheel

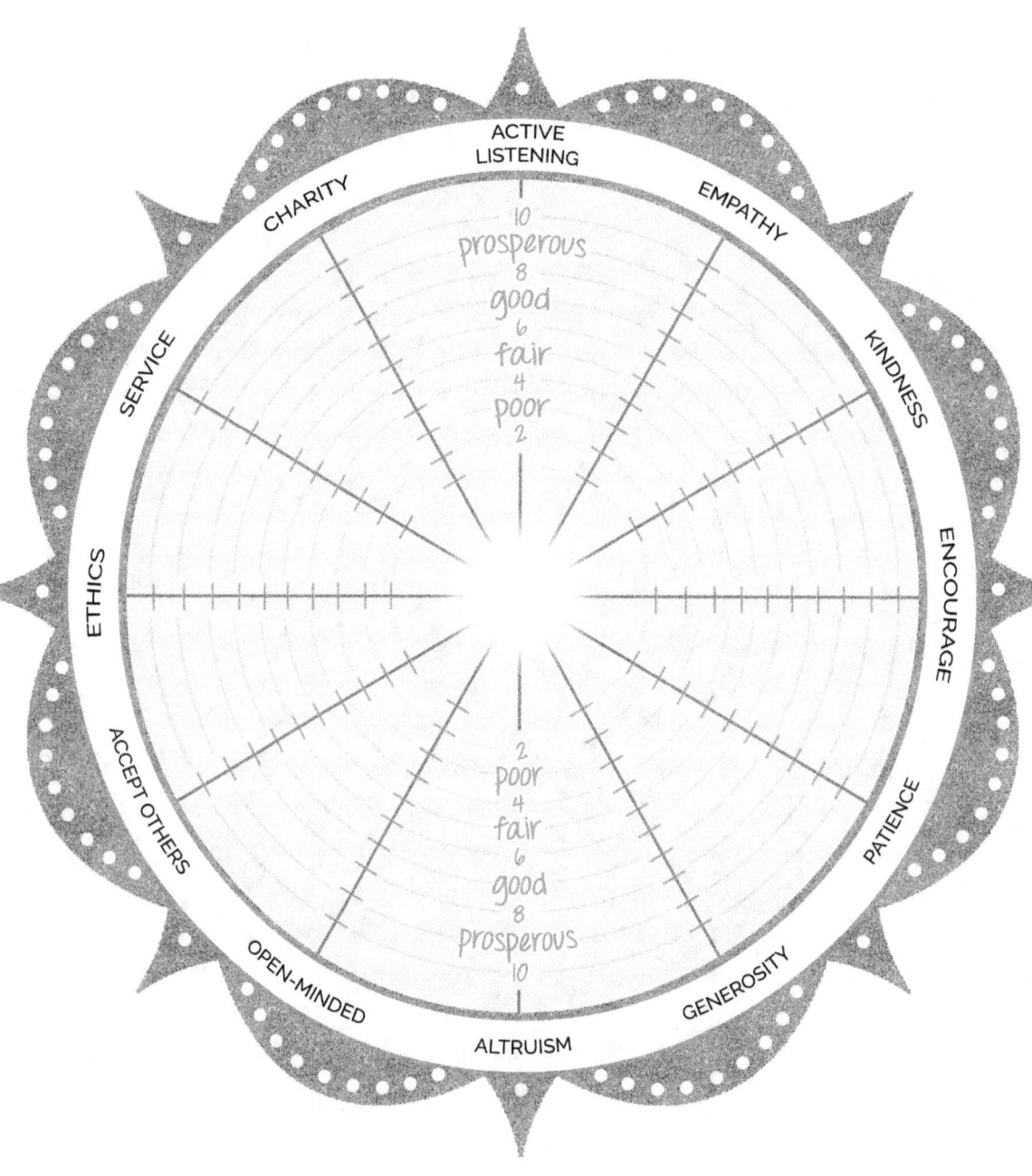

The Compassion Wheel

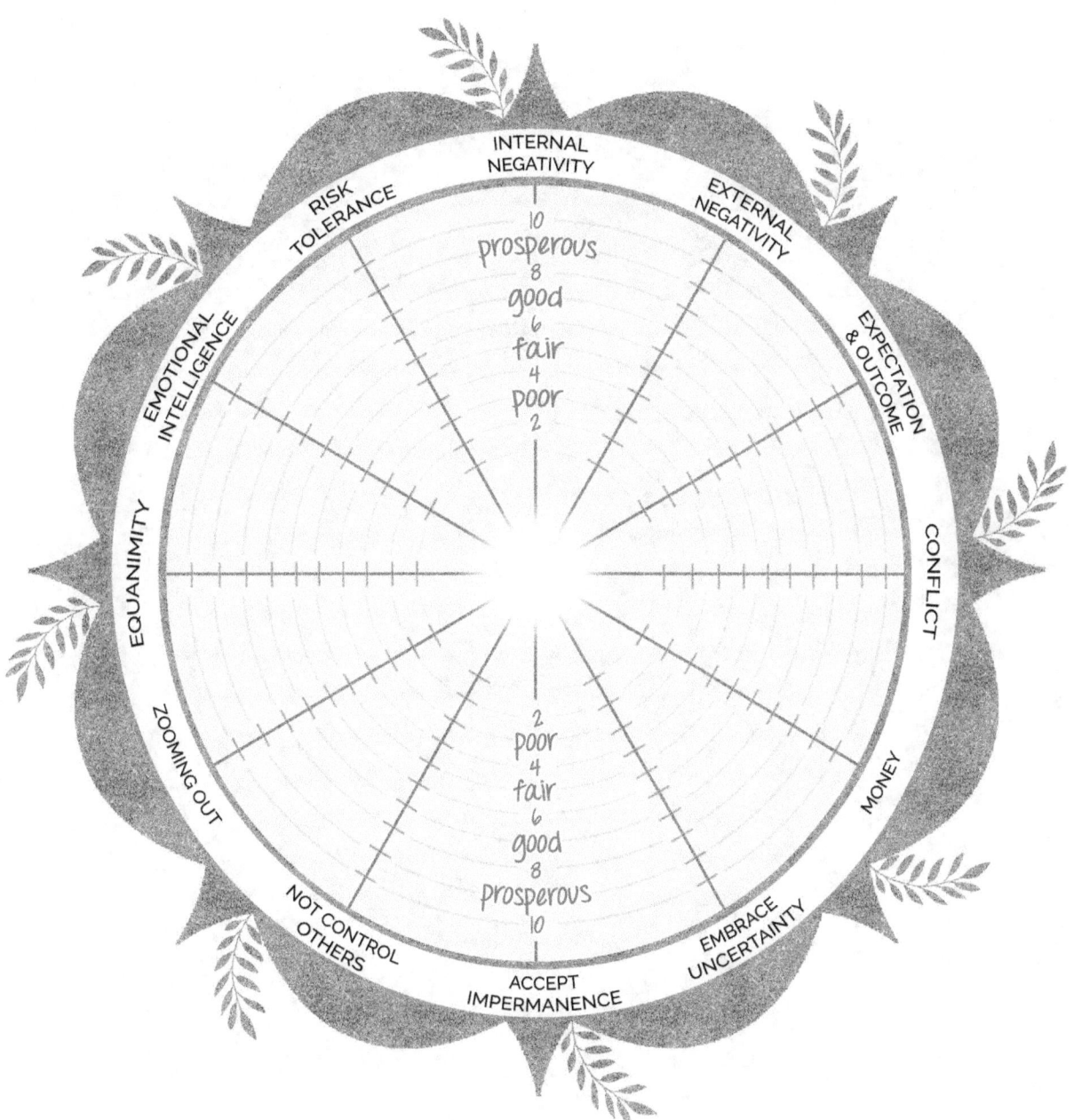

The Detachment Wheel

Joyce Marter, LCPC, CSP®

The Positivity Wheel

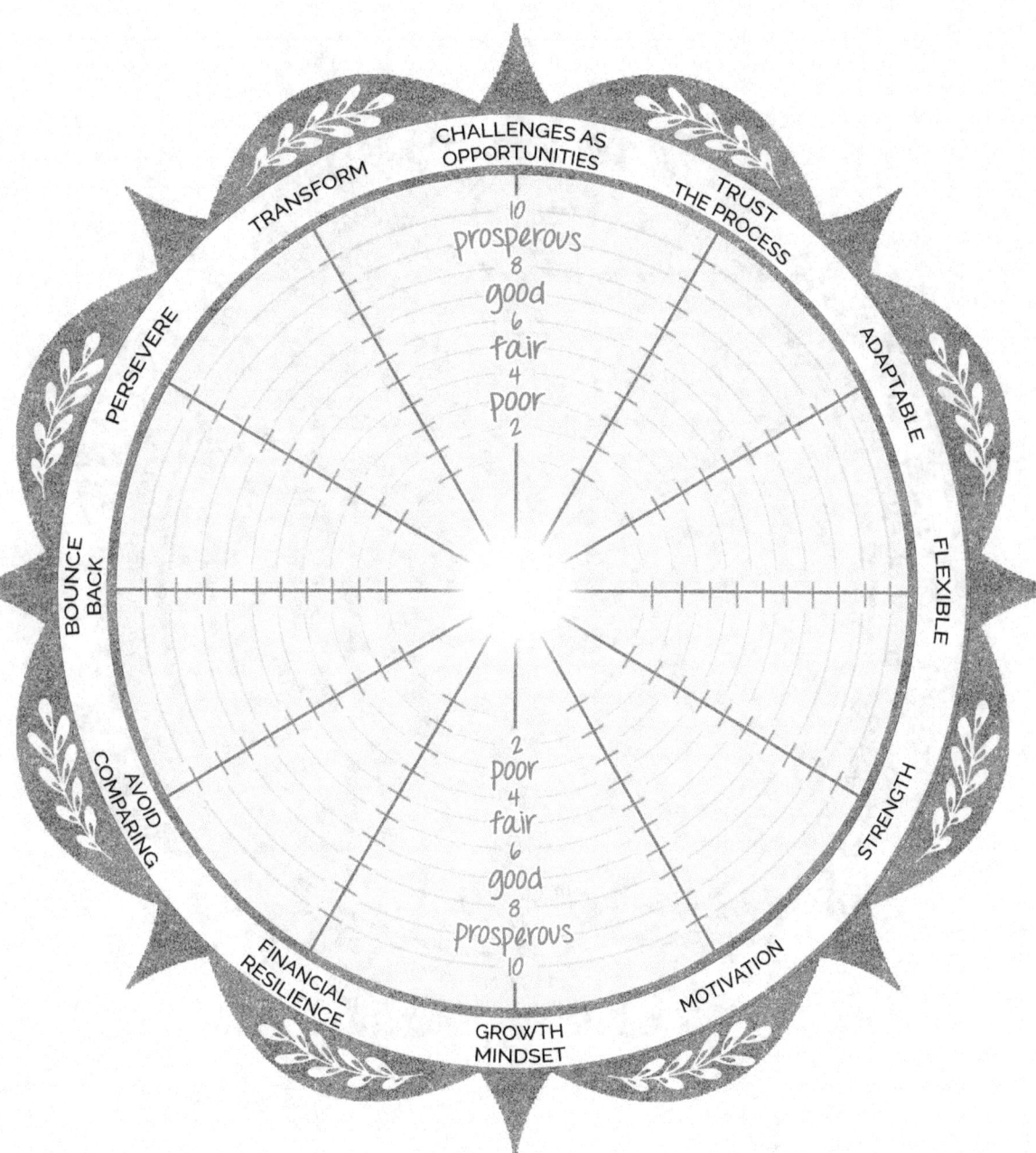

The Resilience Wheel

The Mindset Fix Wheel

NOTES

As you use this workbook, you may want to jot things down, or give yourself a reminder to revisit certain chapters in the future. The following pages are here for you to use in making the Financial Mindset Fix and ongoing component of your life.

CHAPTER 1 NOTES

CHAPTER 2 NOTES

CHAPTER 3 NOTES

_____

_____

_____

_____

_____

_____

_____

_____

_____

_____

_____

_____

_____

_____

_____

_____

_____

_____

_____

_____

_____

_____

CHAPTER 4 NOTES

CHAPTER 5 NOTES

CHAPTER 6 NOTES

Joyce Marter, LCPC, CSP®

CHAPTER 7 NOTES

_____

_____

_____

_____

_____

_____

_____

_____

_____

_____

_____

_____

_____

_____

_____

_____

_____

_____

_____

_____

_____

_____

CHAPTER 8 NOTES

CHAPTER 9 NOTES

CHAPTER 10 NOTES

CHAPTER 11 NOTES

CHAPTER 12 NOTES

_____

_____

_____

_____

_____

_____

_____

_____

_____

_____

_____

_____

_____

_____

_____

_____

_____

_____

_____

_____

ABOUT THE AUTHOR

Joyce Marter, LCPC, CSP®, widely recognized as "America's Workplace Therapist," is a licensed psychotherapist, entrepreneur, professional speaker, author, and media contributor dedicated to empowering others to reach their full potential. With over 25 years of clinical experience and over 20 of professional speaking and training, she is the go-to expert for mental health, financial mindset and holistic success.

Joyce Marter, LCPC, CSP®

In 2004, Joyce founded Urban Balance, a counseling practice that expanded to over 100 clinicians across ten locations in three states during her 13-year tenure as CEO. She successfully sold the company in 2017 to focus on her passion for writing and speaking.

As a globally renowned Certified Speaking Professional (CSP®), Joyce has collaborated with organizations, businesses, associations, universities, and corporations of all sizes to destigmatize mental health issues, facilitate corporate wellness, and promote work-life balance, as well as mental and financial health among individuals, leaders and teams.

She has been elected to serve a three-year term (2025–2028) on the Board of Directors of the National Speakers Association, where she has been a member since 2018. For 15 years, Joyce served as adjunct faculty at The Family Institute at Northwestern University and has held four board presidencies on state and regional professional counseling organizations.

A sought-after media expert, Joyce is a resident contributor for Forbes, Psychology Today, MoneyGeek, and other platforms. She reaches a global media audience of over 1.2 billion people annually, with features in The Wall Street Journal, MSN, CNN, Inc., MTV, and other top-tier outlets.

Her book, *The Financial Mindset Fix: A Mental Fitness Program for an Abundant Life*, has been published in four languages, has received eight book awards and six honorable mentions in book festivals across the globe.

Joyce and her husband, Jason Marotzke, reside in Cape Coral, FL, and have a blended family that includes four adult children, a granddaughter named Evelyn, and two chihuahuas. She leads a vibrant life filled with travel, treasured friendships, and time spent in nature and play.

Joyce is a Founding Member of the Cape Coral Women for Good Giving Circle and a monthly donor to organizations such as The National Alliance on Mental Illness, The Human Rights Campaign, Days for Girls International, and The Tanzanian Children's Fund.

Through her dynamic speaking engagements, coaching, consulting, and writing, Joyce Marter continues to inspire and guide individuals and organizations toward achieving greater personal and professional prosperity.

Joyce knows it is her life's purpose to remove the shame and stigma surrounding mental health and financial stress and to provide people with practical tools to heal, recover, thrive and prosper.

Scan now and unlock Marty's life changing Online Course!